Y0-CDN-436

SUNSHINE/NOIR
writing from san diego and tijuana

JIM MILLER, EDITOR

SAN DIEGO WRITERS COLLECTIVE

SAN DIEGO CITY WORKS PRESS
SAN DIEGO, CALIFORNIA

Copyright © 2005 San Diego City Works Press

All rights reserved. Authors of individual pieces retain copyright to their pieces. No part of this book may be reproduced in any form without written permission from the publisher and/or the authors of the individual pieces.

Permissions acknowledgements can be found in the back of the book.

ISBN 0-9765801-0-1

Library of Congress Control Number 2005901269

San Diego City Works Press is a non-profit press, funded by local writers and friends of the arts, committed to the publication of fiction, poetry, creative nonfiction, and art by members of the San Diego City College community and the community at large. For more about San Diego City Works Press please visit our website at www.cityworkspress.org.

Cover Painting "The End." by Perry Vasquez

Published in the United States by San Diego City Works Press, California

Printed in the United States of America

Acknowledgements

The San Diego Writers Collective is extremely indebted to the American Federation of Teachers, Local 1931, without whose generous contribution, this book would not be possible.

We are also greatly indebted to Mark Dubofsky and Jazz 88 (KSDS 88.3) for helping us promote this work, and to San Diego City College and the San Diego City College Foundation for giving us a home.

Also, without the advice of the people at Heyday Press, the founding of San Diego City Works Press would have been much more difficult. The support and partnership of WORD San Diego and Voz Alta have helped get us off the ground. We would also like to thank the following individuals for their labor and/or contributions to the press: Adam Bogage, Alan Taylor, and Winston Butler.

Table of Contents

Introduction: Searching for Literary San Diego

"Historically, it seems, San Diego cannot represent itself, and is barely represented by others."
David Reid on literary San Diego

In 1896, Theosophist Katherine Tingley had a dream of "a white city in a golden land by the sundown sea," which she came to associate with the gleaming coast of San Diego, California. Tingley's visionary imagination was a nice complement to the inflated mythology penned by the city's boosters, but not all observers fell in line with the sun-drenched utopianism of the Anglo elite. In 1932, Edmund Wilson labeled San Diego "The Jumping-Off Place" as a result of its nation-leading suicide rate. The city, it appeared to Wilson, promised liberation but could only deliver a chimera of false hope for the sick and economically devastated. Three years after Wilson's seminal essay, the narrator in Max Miller's *The Man on the Barge*, noting the "march of pain" of desperately ill sun worshippers, dryly commented on the unspoken alienation under the azure sky by saying, "Nothing often happened here except the sun."

In the decades following the thirties, San Diego was virtually absent from the world of serious literature, seemingly existing only as a unique setting for the occasional mystery or pulp novel. Even though the city is now home to a number of prominent writers, the idea of a literary culture still seems like an alien and improbable notion to many San Diegans. Perhaps the suffocating banality of official San Diego's pious "America's Finest City" mantra has led even those who know better to think that nothing is possible here other than the affectless pleasure that comes from drifting back and forth between the beach and the mall. Nonetheless, underneath San Diego's superficial postcard sunshine, writers have found both grit and genuine transcendence. Perhaps the city is best captured by the incongruous juxtaposition of the evanescent beauty of the gleaming coast with the muted gray façade of America's multi-billion dollar killing machine. San Diego is also the sex oozing from the teeming Pacific Beach boardwalk in mid-summer and the lonely deaths of migrants in the unforgiving winter desert. San Diego is neither beyond alienation, nor devoid of ecstasy. It is both Sunshine and Noir.

San Diego is the Anglo Mission fantasy that evolved from the days of Helen Hunt Jackson's *Ramona* and the place where Henry James wrote, "the sense of the shining social and human inane is utter." San Diego is where Henry Miller was converted to free love and radicalism by famous anarchist Emma Goldman on the way to a Tijuana brothel, and the place where right-wing vigilantes tortured and murdered Wobblies for speaking on soapboxes at the corner of 5th and E. America's seventh largest city has produced a minor noir tradition and a sizable canon of gay sailor pulp novels. In the 1890s, Thomas and Anna Fitch saw Coronado as a suitable location for testing a doomsday weapon in *Better Days: Or, the Millionaire of To-morrow,* and in 1959, Raymond Chandler drank himself to death in La Jolla, a place he described as "nothing but a climate." Carey McWilliams chronicled the free speech fight in the first part of the twentieth century, and, from the 1960s to the 1980s, journalist Harold Keen was the most insightful observer of San Diego, deftly portraying the racial turmoil, political corruption, and labor unrest that simmered underneath the glossy "America's Finest City" veneer. Even Bruce Springsteen got in the act in the nineties, adding "Balboa Park," his Guthrie-esque story of the lives of homeless child prostitutes, to his album *The Ghost of Tom Joad.*

In the 1960s, an aging Herbert Marcuse was strolling the local beaches and musing about *One Dimensional Man* while the youthful Cameron Crowe was cranking out rock journalism for *Rolling Stone.* San Diego is described in Thomas Pynchon's *Vineland* (1990) as the home of the mythical "College of the Surf" and its neighboring countercultural enclave:

> Against the somber military blankness at its back, here was a lively beachhead of drugs, sex, and rock n' roll, the strains of subversive music day and night, accompanied by tambourines and harmonicas, reaching like fog through the fence, up the dry gulches and past the sentinel antennas, the white dishes and masts, the steel equipment sheds, finding the ears of sentries attenuated but ominous, like hostile-native sounds in movies about white men fighting savage tribes.

While the halcyon days of the late sixties counterculture may be long gone, those who yearn for a home-grown culture not dominated by a narrative written by real estate developers and public relations specialists might still feel a bit like the savages on the outside of the military industrial complex/theme park that the city's old guard insists defines San Diego. That and the highly trumpeted virtue of "not being Los Angeles" have sufficed for so many years as the city's primary markers of identity that the cultural imagination of San Diego sometimes seems ossified. San Diego has produced everything from *The Wizard of Oz* to cyberpunk novels about biotechnology, but it still has a hard time imagining itself as the diverse, complex, and, at times, absurd comedy and tragedy that it is. We insist upon the sunshine while ignoring the noir, like a politician sticking to his talking points.

Contemporary San Diego maintains its paradoxical sunshine and noir identity, but as the city has grown, it has become increasingly difficult for the boosters to conceal its ugly corners. An old bumpersticker used to express beach chauvinism by proclaiming: "There is no life east of I-5." In 2005, however, the life east of Interstate 5 (the highway that cordons off the beach communities and downtown from the rest of the inland areas) has made itself known and is changing the face of the city. San Diego today is one of the most ethnically diverse cities in the United States. It also has the largest gap between the rich and poor in California and juxtaposes a carefree postcard reality with a massive military industrial complex and an increasingly fortified international border. San Diego County goes from the desert to the sea, contains mountains, wild spaces and the sprawling suburbs which threaten them. In many ways, it is a region on the cutting edge of the Pacific Rim. Still, no major literary culture has evolved despite the large numbers of novelists, poets, and nonfiction writers who live and work in the area. In sum, San Diego is a city in need of a literary voice, a cultural identity that goes beyond the Zoo, Sea World, the beach, and the Super Bowl. *Sunshine/Noir* is an effort to address this need and expose the true face of "the other San Diego."

This anthology presents the reader with a wide range of contemporary San Diego writers of fiction and nonfiction alike as well as poets, artists and photographers. It explores San Diego and Tijuana's border culture; San Diego's multiple identities and lost history; the city's natural beauty and endangered ecologies; its role as a center of the culture of war; and San Diego writers' attempts to explore the meaning of place. By using a multicultural, multidisciplinary, pan-artistic approach, this anthology offers the reader a fresh look at a city yet to be explored in such a fashion. *Sunshine/Noir* is not comprehensive, but rather stands only as a beginning exploration of literary San Diego that leaves many borders yet to be crossed. A partial list of contributors includes Mike Davis, Marilyn Chin, David Reid, Steve Kowit, Jimmy Santiago Baca, Sandra Alcosser, Mark Dery, minerva, Angela Boyce, Harold Jaffe, Adrian Arancibia of the Taco Shop Poets, and many more locals, expatriates, and frequent visitors.

Sunshine/Noir is the product of several years of labor on the part of the San Diego Writers Collective to create San Diego City Works Press. The San Diego Writers Collective is a group of San Diego writers, poets, artists, and patrons dedicated to the publication and promotion of the work of San Diego area artists of all sorts. Our specific interests include local, ethnic, and border writing as well as formal innovation and progressive politics. The Collective's main focus is local, but we are open to occasional collaborations with writers from around the world. City Works Press is a non-profit press, funded by local writers and friends of the arts, committed to the publication of fiction, poetry, creative nonfiction, and art by members of the San Diego City College community and the community at large. For more about San Diego City Works Press please visit our website at www.cityworkspress.org.

Jim Miller
San Diego Writers Collective
San Diego City Works Press

Migra Mouse

Photo by Perry Vasquez

BORDER CROSSINGS

Photo by Perry Vasquez

*"one small patch for man
one giant patch for mankind"*

THE KEEP ON CROSSIN' PROJECT

"Keep on Crossin..." is a political provocation aimed at the heart of the California experience. Did I say heart? I really mean cora-zon. Ever since Eureka became our state motto, waves of immi-grants have crossed these borders to pursue a piece of the dream as they understand it. In the process they have added their laugh-ter and tears to the drama of our common history.

In honor of those innumerable crossings we offer this icon as a kind of mascot for the crossing masses. His name: **R. Carumba**. His journey begins in a land both far away and close at hand. If you happen to meet him in the street some day, treat him with respect. He brings mojo to all good girls and boys who believe in his eternal wisdom.

Victor Payan and Perry Vasquez

Keep on Crossin' Manifesto

When in the course of human events it becomes necessary to cross borders of political, social, linguistic, cultural, economic and technological construction...we will cross. For long before there were borders, there were crossers. We are the proud sons and daughters of these crossers, and we hold that crossing is a basic human right. Furthermore, we hold this right to be in-illegal alienable.

Artificial borders of body and mind and spirit must be crossed off the list. For every star-crossed, cross-bearing, cross-platform, cross-dressing, cross-country, cross-walker at the crossroads of culture, the time has come to cross.

We are living in a time when a truckload of toxic waste has more rights to cross than a human being. Wherever and whenever this is the case, we will cross.

Our crossing will be a sign to other crossers that the time has come to cross. We will cross at intersections. Anywhere we cross will become an intersection by the act of our crossing. We will look both ways before crossing, and then, with the positive momentum of humanity, we will cross.

We will cross into other manifestos. These include but are not limited to the Prague Manifesto for Esperanto, the Russell-Einstein Manifesto against nuclear war, the Roxy Music song "Manifesto," the Universal Declaration of Human Rights, the Plan of Delano, the Plan Espiritual de Aztlan and any other plans, declarations or manifestos that encourage, promote and reward crossing.

When the border expands, we contract. And when the border contracts, we expand. And when it is time to cross, we will cross all by ourselves.

Wherever there are tired, huddled masses yearning to breathe free, we will cross.

Wherever there's a cop beatin' up a guy, we will cross.

As Martin Luther King wrote from the injustice stained confines of a Birmingham jail: "We are caught in an inescapable network of mutuality, tied in a single garment of destiny."

By wearing this patch, we declare that our garment be counted as a piece from Dr. King's "single garment of destiny."

And to ensure that the sun and moon continue to shine on the smiling faces of the free, we will keep on crossing.

Manifiesto Keep on Crossin'

Cuando en el transcurso de los acontecimientos humanos se hace necesario cruzar fronteras de construcción política, social, lingüística, cultural, económica y tecnológica... cruzaremos. Mucho antes de que hubiera fronteras hubo cruzantes. Somos los orgullosos hijos e hijas de aquellos cruzantes y sostenemos que el cruce es un derecho humano fundamental. Aún más, sostenemos que este derecho es inagenable.

Crucemos de la lista las fronteras artificiales del cuerpo y el pensamiento y el espíritu. Para cada trans-humante, trans-gresor, trans-vestido, trans-portado viviendo en la encrucijada de la cultura, ha llegado la hora de cruzar.

Vivimos en una época en la que un cargamento de vertidos tóxicos tiene más derecho al cruce que un ser humano. Cuando sea y cualquiera que sea el caso, cruzaremos.

Nuestro cruce será una señal para otros cruzantes que ha llegado la hora de cruzar. Cruzaremos en los cruces. Cualquier lugar que crucemos se convertirá en cruce por la acción misma de nuestro cruce. Antes de cruzar, miraremos a ambos lados y luego, con el impulso positivo de la humanidad, cruzaremos.

Nos cruzaremos con otros manifiestos. Éstos incluyen, pero no se limitan, al Manifiesto de Praga a favor del esperanto, el Manifiesto Russell-Einstein en contra de la guerra nuclear, la canción "Manifiesto" de Roxy Music, la Declaración Universal de los Derechos Humanos, el Plan de Delano, el Plan Espiritual de Aztlán o cualquieres otros planes, declaraciones o manifiestos que animen, inciten o recompensen el cruce.

Cuando la frontera se expande, nosotros nos contraemos. Y cuando la frontera se contrae, nosotros nos expandimos. Y cuando sea la hora de cruzar, cruzaremos automaticamente.

Donde haya masas cansadas, amontonadas, ansiando respirar libremente, cruzaremos.

Donde haya un poli dando una golpiza a un tipo, cruzaremos.

Como escribió Martin Luther King desde los confines de la cárcel de Birmingham, teñidos por la injusticia: "Estamos atrapados en una red ineludible de mutualidad, unidos en la prenda única del destino."

Al llevar este parche, declaramos que nuestra ropa cuenta como una de esas "prendas únicas del destino" de que habló el Dr. King.

Y para asegurar que el sol y la luna sigan brillando sobre los rostros sonrientes de los seres libres, seguimos cruzando.

Photo by Michael Mesa

Altar

Jimmy Santiago Baca

Bull's Blood

Franklin rose early on Saturday morning, made himself a cup of coffee and toast, and after eating, went into the garage. He grabbed a box off the dwindling stack and carried it into his study. Almost three months after he and Lynn had bought their house, he hoped to finally finish unpacking, and with a mixture of relief and annoyance that this was how he was spending his Saturday morning, he began sorting through the religious statues, paperback novels, poetry books, family photographs, old tax returns, and receipts. Most of this he threw in the trash pile. Then he opened a manila envelope and smiled when he saw what it contained: a photograph showing both of them covered in blood, taken six years before, after he first met Lynn.

A year before the photograph was taken, Franklin was still married. He was hurt but not surprised when his wife informed him that she had filed for divorce. They'd been having problems for three years, and he never really had faith that he could make it work. Something inside him had given up because none of his efforts had succeeded—marital counseling, individual therapy, and other remedies all failed to improve their relationship. He was thirty-nine and played bass guitar and congas in a salsa band; at the same time that his nine-year marriage dissolved, the band disintegrated and his close friends moved away. Of the ones that remained, two killed themselves and the rest became complacent—all they wanted out of life was to have enough people for volleyball and a barbecue at the park on Sunday.

The same weekend his wife informed him she had filed, he packed his clothes in boxes, put them in his pickup, and drove away with one last sight of her in his rearview mirror: standing in the yard, a glazed rage in her eyes and a scowl on her face. He left her everything—house, car, furniture, and appliances. He knew that he would never marry again because it would inevitably end for some horrible reason—something unseen, unplanned, but lurking there in the dark, in the near future, waiting for the right time to spring out at him and shatter his trust.

He never fully understood why his marriage soured, but he tried to accept that that's how life was: One day the good things—commitment, laughter, love, passion—were there, and the next, poof!, they were gone, leaving a residue of misery staining everything he looked at.

The work he had put into making a good life for his family never went the way it should have, and he felt that he was not good at the ups and downs of marriage, not good at sitting down and discussing what was on his wife's mind—things that mattered and which he now assumed might have salvaged his relationship.

But it wasn't in his nature to change, to take on another way of listening and acting and living, another way of caring and being with someone. He was too afraid—to wander in the dark, groping here and there, hoping his lover's hand would be there when he needed it. He could only go on as he was, and perhaps one day he and his wife could sit across from each other at a table in a coffee shop and simply talk, two acquaintances with mutual respect. He didn't believe in happiness but he could settle for stability, an unchanging continuum with no surprises.

But Franklin underestimated the damage the breakup would do to him. He rented a second-floor, two-room apartment downtown, with sliding doors on a balcony that opened to a park across the street, and while his ex-wife traveled and vacationed as if she were free and sixteen again, he spent his days listlessly pacing from one room to the other, leaning his elbows on the balcony railing, watching couples and retirees walk their dogs and come and go in the park until it was late and he went to sleep on his futon mattress on the floor.

He felt incapable of stepping outside his door and engaging anyone on any level for any reason. Over the next few weeks he became more isolated and grew increasingly bereft and melancholy.

On the day Franklin turned forty, he found himself reviewing his life. He bleakly admitted to himself that it amounted to very little. Like his former friends' lives, his was mediocre at best, and now he felt pulled down by an undertow of despair. He thought briefly about going to night school for computer programming, accounting, or real estate, but persistent inertia paralyzed him— something deep inside him was growing more and more afraid. He was falling apart, and how deep into the abyss he was going to nosedive he didn't know.

* * *

Six months before he met Lynn, he had closed himself in his apartment and started drinking gin and experimenting with drugs. He began to have thoughts of killing himself. He was haunted by the possibility that his life would always be like this, and the razor-sharp slivers of fear punctured the edges of his mind at all hours, intruding into his dreams and thoughts as he looked at people passing below his balcony or heard them step ponderously in the hallway past his door. He had even called his dealer to ask him to bring over a pistol along with his next delivery. He later eyed the pistol lying on the coffee table, luring him to try the ultimate high; he guessed that if he got drunk or high enough, the odds of his taking his own life were better than fifty-fifty.

He abandoned basic hygiene and walked around in boxers and a T-shirt, unshaved and unwashed. His attempt at socializing was to drink every night at the corner bar, and he became a prolific womanizer. He wanted to enjoy as many women in as many ways as possible and not think about where his life was going or how it might end. One young prostitute believed he had been bewitched and that evil spirits inhabited him, and he believed her but could do nothing about it. He resigned himself to living under the pall of damnation. To his mind, this was justification for his ongoing self-destruction.

* * *

Perhaps because of the elevation or from the fatigue after having driven twelve hundred miles from New Mexico to Salt Lake City, the beer hit Franklin harder than usual. He was on his sixth cup, sitting in the arena next to his cousin Louis, who had been eliminated earlier in the saddle bronc category at the Salt Lake City national rodeo finals.

A huge theater screen suspended from the coliseum ceiling flashed the next event: the women's barrel racing finals. The screen showed the contestants—pretty, ponytailed blond and brunette cowgirls with strong, sensuous, compact bodies.

Franklin didn't expect to be enjoying himself, but now that he was here he silently thanked his cousin, who had forced him to come. A few days before, Louis had run into Franklin's ex-wife at the grocery store, and she told him about Franklin's bizarre behavior—his refusal to answer the door or the telephone, the boozing, the womanizing, the drugs—his overall descent into hell. Later Louis went over to Franklin's, without even inquiring whether he wanted some company, and ordered, "You're going to get some fresh air, see some pretty women, and party with me—get your stuff, we're leaving."

Before Franklin could make a sound, Louis choked off any protest with a forearm under Franklin's chin, pinning him against the wall, commanding, "I'm inviting you to a party, and I don't aim to be turned down by family. Get on it now 'fore I put a boot up that ass!"

At the rodeo, Franklin couldn't help but smile as he watched Louis get crushed like a bag of potato chips by a crazed, man-killing bull and, in another competition, stamped in the dust by a red-eyed bucking bronc. To witness healthy men and women, seemingly of sound mind, put their lives on the line for eight seconds gave him a reprieve from his own self-destructive habits and pulled him out of his dark mood. As he saw it, they were even crazier than he was.

There were reporters on the bleachers all around him with rucksacks filled with notepads, tape recorders, and cameras, sipping from whiskey flasks, putting the previous days' interview notes in order. Tilting his head back to gulp the last swig of beer from his paper cup, out of the corner of his eye Franklin saw a woman's face flash across the giant movie screen that hung from the coliseum canopy. At first he thought his eyes were playing tricks on him. The cup fell out of his hand, beer dribbled from the corners of his lips, and he coughed on the liquid that went down his windpipe. Regaining his composure, he wiped his eyes and mouth and studied the screen, but the woman was gone. He must have only imagined, for an instant, the most beautiful woman he'd ever seen.

The halftime show started and two cowboys drove trucks with horse trailers into the arena. A cow trotted out from one of the chutes, its milk bag flopping to its gait. A referee whistled and the two cowboys jumped out of their pickups, took out their horses, and saddled them. The first cowboy to successfully mount his horse, lasso the cow, fill a cup with milk, get back on his horse, and race to the finish line, still holding the cup of milk, won. The race took place and then the clowns came out, chasing a Shetland pony with a blue heeler riding it. Some dove at the Shetland while others somersaulted over it. The clowns were ex-bronc riders who couldn't ride anymore because of injuries but still wanted to stay in the scene.

A little later, a tractor flanked by young 4-H cowboys came out and raked the arena smooth. They set up orange drums for the barrel racing competition and departed. A few minutes later, the first horse burst out of the gates and churned around the barrels, hooves spitting dirt puffs. Franklin was amazed at how far down these women riders could lean their horses—a mere five or six inches off the ground—while going that fast around a barrel. He saw the horses wrench sideways, snorting, every muscle strained taut to its limit. He watched in awe as rider after rider blasted out of the gate, determined to be the best.

Then the last young rider, with long walnut-colored hair, flew out of the gate. He looked up at the screen and his lower lip trembled, perspiration beaded on his forehead, and he found it difficult to breathe—he hadn't imagined her after all. She was the same woman he had seen slash by on the screen earlier, and now she took his breath away.

Six years later, as he looked at the photograph he held in his hands, the sight of her bloody face looking up at him still pierced him with its openhearted vow, innocent and truthful as rays of light radiating over water at sunrise.

The initial sight of her had reignited something in him that had died, and it came alive as hot as the blinding camera flashes that flickered from the bleachers that day. All the qualities in a woman that he desired-indeed, fantasized about—he sensed she possessed. He had dreamed of her but had never pictured her face. She was more beautiful than he could have imagined.

As she flew among the barrels, strands of her dark hair flew back with the horse's auburn mane, her tanned almond complexion blended in with the horse's dark coat, and its turquoise halter, reins, and saddle trim merged with her blue eyes. She lost her cowboy hat on the first turn. Like a general charging into battle, she attacked the barrels, at times leaning so low on the turns that her reins grazed the ground. Franklin had never experienced such desire for any woman, and watching her performance on the edge of his seat, he joined the crowd to roar her on.

The times were announced immediately after each run, and after hers the announcer stated that five seconds had been subtracted from her overall time as a penalty for knocking down a barrel. It was enough to drop her to fourth. He saw her walking to the rear of the coliseum where the horses were stalled, watching closely to see if anyone met her. She was alone. Franklin hurried down the stands. He spotted her heading to the open-air stalls, and as he neared her, he started worrying that she would think he was a nut. But what could he do?

And then suddenly he was beside her, gulping for air. The sight of her big blue eyes, high cheekbones, and shapely lips stunned him almost speechless.

She glanced at him suspiciously and said, "Can I help you with something?" Her voice sounded light and yet powerful. He struggled to make himself relevant.

"No, no, well, yes...uhh—Lynn, right?—you did great..." Franklin said.

"Yeah, he did okay," she said, petting her horse, "it was my leg that knocked over that barrel." Her horse was beautiful—a black gelding, half quarter horse, half thoroughbred, it had four white stockings and a blaze of white down its face.

All around them penned-up livestock bellowed, whinnied, and bleated, and the humid air reeked of dung and horse sweat. Yet, because he was gazing at Lynn, to Franklin the encounter seemed as sweetly romantic as a snowy evening in a mountain cabin.

Lynn faced him with dust-caked cheeks, streaked where she had wiped away her tears. "What is it you want?" she asked, making an effort to sound cheerful.

"Five seconds, that's all you lost by. But you were the best...the very best."

She searched his face. "My horse might be poor, but he did good, it was my fault." She flushed with emotion and it took all her composure to keep from weeping.

"Can I walk back with you?" He paused. "This might sound crazy, but when I saw you, a part of me remembered you, as if you were someone I had known for a long time."

She gave him a long look as if to determine whether she could trust him. "Sure; right now I feel like the loneliest cowgirl in this whole rodeo."

* * *

Lynn called his hotel the following morning and they went out for breakfast. She had no expectations, but when she saw Franklin leaning against the red brick restaurant a sparkling sensation overcame her. As she crossed the street, though it was a warm April day, snowflakes started to float down softly. Later, when she was alone and thoughtful, she would interpret the snowfall as a heavenly omen in their favor.

From that moment on they could hardly stand being apart. They felt a history not yet lived awaiting them. And this certainty expanded and brimmed in all their senses, like the fragrant aroma of homemade bread just pulled from a brick oven. Days and nights blurred by. They gradually put their past lives behind them and in a short while it seemed they hardly even recognized who they had been, as if they had been wearing costumes until then, pretending to be people they were not.

Still, there were times Lynn agonized over what people said and thought about them: She was twenty years old, he was forty; she was white, he was Hispanic; he was Catholic, she was Mormon, and she'd been groomed by church elders to follow the

Latter Day Saints life and marry someone condoned by the church officials. When she went home to visit her parents, they threatened to disown her if she didn't come to her senses and discontinue her affair with Franklin. "He's only five years younger than I am," her father roared at the kitchen table. Her girlfriends, over drinks at the old college watering hole, guessed he was suffering a midlife crisis and advised Lynn to take advantage of it—have all the sex she wanted with him, travel, buy clothes, accept his money, then leave him. She was torn in two because she knew her parents and friends were probably right, but she loved Franklin beyond all understanding. No matter what adversity they had to face, they would take on each challenge together.

Franklin's friends were highly critical of him too; some accused him of thinking he was too good for his own kind. They mocked him for being a "coconut"—brown on the outside, white on the inside. But beyond what friends and family said, society gave the harshest condemnation.

When Lynn and Franklin relaxed in the whirlpool at the gym, women turned their contemptuous eyes on Lynn for being a young woman with an older man. In restaurants in the ski resorts north of Salt Lake City, white people glared at Franklin for daring to claim the company of a young white girl. In southern New Mexico, in cafés packed with Chicanos, customers scrutinized them and smirked, inferring that she was merely his temporary sex toy and he was a foolish man without scruples. Wherever they went in public, bigotry followed them, but in private nothing could lessen their romantic exhilaration.

Lynn had set out to get Franklin healthy again and soon had him jogging with her. They ran along the West Mesa dunes, where rattlesnakes and coyotes greeted them as they scaled the dormant volcano. He puffed and coughed and she had to wait for him to catch up, but gradually he was running next to her. Along with juices made from fruits, vegetables, and wheat grass, she had him drink six glasses of water a day, and she fixed him robust salads. After he quit smoking, she taught him how to swim at the gym pool, and later, after swimming, they strolled along the Rio Grande, surrounded by willows, and meditated on the flowers, the flowing water, and the cranes wading in the shallows. Sometimes she would dance wildly in a clearing, captivating him with her gyrating, hypnotic mating ritual, and then they would make love on the ground.

These were emotionally packed days, grounded in a way Franklin had not enjoyed before. Being with Lynn had renewed his belief in God and given him a newfound faith in his ability to create a meaningful relationship. During this time, on the way back from a three-day camping trip, they stopped in at St. Francis Cathedral in Santa Fe. A dozen or so elderly parishioners were sitting in pews counting Hail Marys on rosaries when Franklin and Lynn entered and took a seat nearest the main altar. Franklin closed his eyes and when he opened them a few minutes later, he saw Lynn crying, overwhelmed with piety. Then she stood, went up to the communion railing, raised her arms, and began to pray aloud. The people around her stared as she thanked Christ for bringing Franklin and her together. When they left the church, Franklin asked her what had happened. Lynn said that she had had a religious experience and planned to convert to Catholicism.

They headed to a café off the plaza, and as she talked avidly about her encounter with the spirit of Christ, which she had felt infuse her being, Franklin gave a silent prayer of his own: that God would give him the faith he needed to make the relationship work. Privately, he was still afraid love would blow up in his face again.

As summer ended they took long drives into the country, along prairie roads bordered with rolling meadows and narrow blacktop roads winding through forested mountains. During one trip Franklin told Lynn that he thought most men in their forties stopped trying to achieve the dreams they had as young men. Before he had met her, he said, he had been stuck midstream, unable to find the strength to reach the other bank, with no connections to anything worthy of belief—the spirituality movements he had sought out seemed too trendy and shallow and lacking in compassion. But now, for the first time in a long time, with Lynn's love, he possessed the strength to cross the stream and believe in people and life again.

In September the two found themselves in Washington, D.C., where Franklin had a weeklong job playing congas at a salsa club. One Saturday morning they drove to a frozen lake. Franklin picked up a large stone and threw it as far as he could onto the ice.

"I'll prove how much I love you," he told Lynn, and started out on the lake to retrieve the rock. She watched quietly with her big blue eyes tracking his every breath and step. When he finally reached the rock and picked it up, the ice began cracking all around him. He couldn't turn around, so he stood there, looking out over the frozen lake, wondering what would happen if it broke and he sank in. He carried the rock walking backward. Each step he took made the ice break more, fragments floated apart, bubbles gurgled beneath the thinned ice, and crack lines spidered all around like a huge white web slowly ensnaring him. Franklin remained calm as he felt the ice crackling and moving up and down. Five or six yards from the shore, the ice finally gave way and broke, and he fell into the slushy water—water so cold it would freeze him to the bone in seconds. But before he was completely swallowed up by the water, he threw the rock onto the shore and managed to crawl his way to firm ground. Blue in the lips and hands, and shivering, but smiling, he managed to chatter the words out, "I love you, Lynn."

Later, in December, Franklin flew home with Lynn to spend Christmas with her parents. Feeling nervous and awkward around her friends one night at a party, he got drunk and drove crazily through the snow-packed streets, speeding through red lights and nearly killing them both. He left the next morning and she didn't return with him. Lynn had never seen this side of Franklin and the incident completely unnerved her.

She said she needed some time to think and that things between them were so intense, she wanted to slow down and get grounded. She called him later to tell him she was going to accept a job offer teaching English. He objected, arguing it would tear them apart, but she insisted it was only temporary. She needed to be around her friends, visit with her parents, and think about their relationship.

He drove around a lot during that period, revisiting the area where he had grown up. His thinking was getting worse and worse, and he now wondered if their time together was nothing more than a cheap affair. At one point she said that her friends would not understand. Understand what, he thought now, that he loved her, that he wanted a life with her?

He wrote to her, saying that he was ready to settle down, that he was prepared to spend his life with her. He didn't care what people thought or said; he promised her he would be true and they would have a good life. But her replies seemed cautious, mistrustful, and emotionally strained. He grew angry and accused her of playing him and his emotions—for her, he said, his love was all a game. This made her withdraw into silence and when he did hear from her again weeks later, she sounded relieved to have her life back to normal. She was back in her old apartment, having coffee with old friends before work and beers with girlfriends after work, and she was content to let their relationship cool off.

Over the next three months, they talked on the phone almost every night. He questioned her about why she was unprepared to commit herself to him and she in turn wondered how stable a life with him would be. She kept returning to the night when he got so drunk. It worried her. They went over the problems they had already encountered because of their age difference and cultural backgrounds. When Lynn asked him how he felt about marriage, again he backed away from saying he would marry her. He was afraid of not being able to measure up to her expectations and he said he wanted to first try living together. With some reservation, she agreed to jump-start their relationship again and flew down to Santa Fe for a weekend with him.

At his apartment, they talked long into the night, speaking truthfully and solemnly about their mutual fear of commitment, of failure, of hurting each other and being hurt. They couldn't articulate the contradiction that struck at the center of their souls: the desire to love and be loved, to give and yet take, to be together and alone, and last, the impulse to be courageous and fearful. Though they both admitted they had never loved anyone so intensely and deeply, perhaps the safest thing to do would be to give each other time and space, and if it was meant to be, they'd end up together. But as soon as they woke, they found that they couldn't stop crying and kissing and holding each other. They were quiet on the way to the airport and they wept as they parted.

Over the next two months they lived in separate worlds, dated other people, worked, and made new friends. They tried to forget each other but it was useless. Franklin called Lynn one day to tell her he had decided to move to Mexico. He left a message on her machine and she called him back that evening.

Lynn said she was due for a break from teaching and agreed to drive down to New Mexico and meet him at the hot springs. He tried to sound nonchalant but his voice broke in places nevertheless.

Sunday morning he rose early, packed a lunch with various fruits, sandwiches, bottled water, and juice, and drove two hours to the hot springs. She looked as beautiful and stunning as she had that first day at the rodeo. It was a perfect day, blue sky, sunshine. At the springs a host of Chicano families was scattered around, and as Franklin and Lynn talked in one of the pools, they watched kids squeal with delight as they ran over the grassy meadows down into the stream to swim and splash. The scalding, mineral-green water made their flesh red and hot, and Franklin soon helped Lynn climb out of the muddy hole so they could rush down to the swiftly moving stream. They clambered precariously over river stones, hollered vigorously as they lay down in the freezing water, endured it for a few minutes, then leaped up and dashed back to the pool, where they sank down to their necks in the hot bubbling water.

They massaged each other, and then Franklin suggested that he hold her up while she floated in his hands. She stretched out, he put his palms under the small of her back for support, and she remained that way for a long time with her eyes closed. Then she did it to him, had him lean back and surrender to her hands under him. Everything but his eyes were underwater and he could hear the bubbles issuing from the earth below him, rising from the molten rock miles under the surface, making its way up thousands of feet to reach his body to caress him and ease him with its nurturing warmth. For a long time he drifted off with his eyes closed, feeling himself float away into particles that glided out into the universe, attaching to the spirit of all creatures and lifeforms. Though neither could explain how, they both felt the power of the water that had flowed up from the center of the earth to bless them and unite them in a mystical resurgence of faith and hope.

"And that was it..." Franklin heard himself whisper, studying the photograph that captured their glazed looks in the hot sun. Early that day they'd been drinking tequila at the Tijuana Hotel, hours before the bullfights. The matadors stayed at the same hotel, and from time to time, one would sweep by on his way to a waiting car, or another would stand on a coffee table in the lobby with an attendant applying last-minute touch-ups to his costume.

Off in a corner beside windows that looked out over a patio garden, he and Lynn were drinking with a Chicano photographer wearing a bull's spine necklace and his boyfriend, the editor of an L.A. magazine. The two men had invited them over to join them in sampling exotic tequilas.

At around one in the afternoon, the four of them, feeling woozy, went out into the heat and headed down the winding cobblestone streets for the arena. The editor talked about how they had met, sharing that he had hired his lover to photograph the matadors. He looked at his companion and gave him a peck on the cheek, saying, "We are the perfect match!"

Lynn and Franklin lost the two men in the hordes of

Mexicans streaming into the coliseum to watch the bullfights. They sat in the first rows, the ones closest to the pit, leaning their elbows on the railing wall so they could see the eyes and expressions of the bulls and matadors up close.

After all the time they had been together, Franklin knew how Lynn's eyes were sometimes the color of green summer sage but changed color depending on what kind of day it was or what clothes she was wearing. On rainy days they were dark green, on windy dry days they became the palest light blue, but on the day he first saw her they were the bluest blue he'd ever seen in his life. It was as if he were looking into the purest coastal waters surrounding an undiscovered island. On the day of the bullfights, they were red as the matador's cape.

Lynn was crying and getting angrier every time a new bull, heralded by the cries of the spectators, proudly broke into the arena and the poised matador bravely faced the bull, lining up his sword under his cape in preparation for battle. After the bull had been stabbed, speared, and ignominiously dragged away, Lynn would rise and scream that it was wrong, that the bull didn't even have a chance. Her hysterics amused the Mexican crowd, who not only found her amusing but, judging by all the flirtatious stares, quite alluring.

Lynn changed her tune with the last bull. They had saved the bravest bull for the final fight, and a hushed awe rose from the spectators as the announcer stated that the bull was unrivaled, the most valiant. Trumpets blared. The bull charged and immediately gored the matador in his thigh. With the matador pulled off to the side so assistants could wrap his wound, the bull snorted around the arena, daring anyone to challenge him. He trotted around as if he were immortal, galloping wildly, swinging his horns, and taunting the crowd to deliver him another victim. The crowd loudly booed and ridiculed the matador, who now had to save face and reappear for the showdown.

Lynn was the loudest, even the cruelest, standing and shouting for the bull to avenge the deaths of the other bulls. But then the crowd grew quiet as the matador walked over to where Franklin and Lynn sat, unleashed his sword from its scabbard, pointed it at Lynn, and bowed. The crowd went berserk again, tossing sombreros in the air, toasting their pulque cups and tequila bottles, while others bowed and waved. Souvenir-selling kids rushed over and gave Lynn free roses, a mariachi trio serenaded her with a song, and one young gentleman gave her a beautiful Mexican cowboy hat, which she put on. One of the Mexicans seated a few feet to Lynn's left leaned over and told

Lynn, "He will kill the bull in your honor! Because you are so beautiful! He's paying homage to your beauty!" Lynn couldn't hear what he said because of the noise from the crowd, nor could she understand what this generous outpouring of affection meant, but as she and Franklin looked around waving back in gratitude, thousands of spectators smiled at them.

The crowd reeled in ecstatic hysteria as huge gates opened up on the far side of the arena and men in uniforms brocaded with glittering jewels came out on horseback with long spears and gradually formed a circle around the bull, surrounding him. The crowd fell deathly silent. Other novice matadors appeared with capes and smaller daggers. The circle tightened around the bull as the creature lunged with false starts in one direction and then another, trying to roll its massive eyes everywhere at once. Confused and alarmed, it charged at matadors wherever it saw them.

Although it could do nothing as daggers and swords plunged into its back and heart and chest, still it did not fall; it refused to go down. Blood drooling from its nose, gushing from its wounds, dribbling in red rivulets down its shimmering black hide, it charged again and again, only to be knifed and speared until the blood literally dripped in a curtain from its wounds and the bull turned red in the lowering sunlight. When it stood in one place, huffing, trying to breathe, pools of blood gathered under its belly. When it moved, scores of daggers planted deep in its muscles jiggled with its movements.

Crying and drinking more tequila, Lynn was yelling her heart out at the cowards when two men dressed in suits descended the bleachers. They escorted Franklin and Lynn up the concrete steps of the arena and around the top of it to the back, and then down into the area where the bulls were dragged after they were killed.

Franklin and Lynn felt disoriented as the two men positioned them under a rough-looking, open-air shed made of four telephone poles and a corrugated roof. Dizzied by too much tequila, the heat, and the roaring crowd, they held hands and waited. They remained as they were, until they heard the crowd give a concerted groan followed by a gasp, then a triumphant howl erupted in deafening celebration.

Seconds later, the big wooden arena doors swung open and a chariot of four horses, breathing foam from their nostrils, charged through dragging the dead bull behind them. Four other men— naked except for ragged and soiled shorts—appeared and unchained the bull that now rested on the ground under the shed.

The bull had not entirely expired and was still snorting out its last heaving breaths, when a giant of a man, wielding a medieval ax, and his cohort, a fierce ash-smudged midget with a sicklelike machete, grabbed Lynn and Franklin and stood them close to the bull.

Lying on its back, its big oval black-and-white eyes glaring and blood streaming from its nostrils and mouth, the bull bellowed mournful grunts as the midget bent down and ripped open the animal's torso from neck to groin. The giant next to him yanked the rib cage apart, and then the midget sank his hand into the bull's chest, held a cup next to a heart artery, and filled it with blood.

He withdrew his hand, turned, and, all spattered and smeared with blood and guts, handed the cup to Lynn, motioning for her to drink. Lynn looked at Franklin, who nodded, and she drank half of it, handing him the other half, which he drained. All the while, just beyond the shed, a mob of Mexicans, Americans, and Asians were shouting and waving fistfuls of money high above their heads, hollering for the testicles, horns, tongue, and penis. The midget stepped toward the crowd, swung his machete in an arc, and yelled that they had better keep their distance. He then cut off a portion of the still warm and beating heart and handed it to Lynn. She bit off a part and chewed and swallowed it. Franklin did the same. They both understood there was no turning back; they had now committed to love and trust each other for life.

Skulls

Photo by Michael Mesa

Adrian Arancibia

mahmoud moves/say somethin' new

mahmoud moves/because...

i just wanted to write
something beautiful
like your teeth
when your lips tire
of holding it all
i wanted a body
becoming a body
with me
with me

believe the 30s the 60s the 90s

say something new

because the fire still burns
because we still can't film
        what they do to us
because we can't ride on the
        trolley without i.d.
because the weeds grow
        and they need to be pulled
because the avocados grow
        and they need to be picked
because we're beat down
        and no one cares
because on certain nights
        the darkness burns
because on certain nights
        bruises darken
because, because...

because windows are still our
        enemies
because we still have to show
        proper i.d. even if we're not driving
because we speak in dialects
        and tongues
because we're thirsty and afraid
        to ask for water

because we're cold and have no one
        to wake us
because we can' unionize
        we can' unionize
but we still believe in miracles

the clap clap clap of thunder
of tracks is not
it's on our arms
it's causing us to die

because it's dead
because we still haven't decided
        to turn our backs
because where we grow
        the night rapes with chemicals
because we want so much to
        fit in
because we're only one marriage away
        from making it
because it's hard
        damn hard

and this becomes the tail end of so much madness

entrails of intestines
intestines as hope
tripas as hope
trips as hope

the day today brought an empty
windshield of views
and sadness of views
and sadness of views

so little to look forward to
so many mornings
with the same panging
feeling on my forehead

and i made believe
it never happened
i made believe it never
happened

made believe my poem
came before soaked
wallabies
wringing moisture from eyes

made believe no matter what
you'd read these lines
these poems without
poetic virtue

and i'm stuck
between floors
and the couple having sex
next door
is circling a whole
through my wall
leaving me alone again

i pretend
you've found a way
of sanctifying this pain
and that some day
i'll look and find
some virtue
in this silence
of a phone held to an ear

no one on the other line
this was my ultimate fear
that my stripped loneliness
moving like a chain at the edge
of a surface
and the rasping sounds
louder and louder
until the night is no longer silent

and silence is noise
and noise is silence

Daniel José Older

Notes from the Border

1.

I didn't know what I'd stepped in. Maybe an old taco, I thought, or, at worst, dog shit. Then I saw my foot on the soft, gray body, the crimson pool forming around it. Oh, the poetry of death. It's almost too easy. I cursed and then cursed again as I tried to scrape gut off my tennis shoe.

2.

This is true.

It's true that the Border Patrol Officer who picked me up wore a bright, well-practiced grin, that his uniform was creased and immaculate, that he drove an unmarked black SUV. It's true that he employed that grin at the most strategic moments in our conversation, like when he informed me that no member of the Border Patrol didn't sympathize with the poor Mexican workers, that the coyotes were the real devils in this game, that the good people of San Diego only wanted what was best for their less fortunate neighbors, and that Operation Gatekeeper had actually lowered the death toll of migrants crossing the border at Tijuana.

"That's strange," I said, "I heard the opposite is true."

"Well, I don't know where you get your info, but you're welcome to look through my statistics file here..."

Our SUV glided smoothly along the rugged border terrain, dipping up and down jagged mountain roads. The wall ran along beside us on into the endless desert. My tour guide's well practiced monologue was suddenly interrupted by a metallic thump on the roof of the SUV and we both whirled our heads around to see a boy running off behind a boulder.

"Yep, they're throwing rocks at us again."

3.

A moment:

Me, the awkward 23 year-old American and Latin but not Latin American, tired and sweaty from a long walk, still a little weary after the three-day train ride from the east coast. I have a passport, an empty apartment and a grant from my college. I'm passing out mayo and salami sandwiches to a cluster of migrants in tattered rags sitting in a sad little circle on a hill of dust a few feet from the border.

Each one has a story. I milk the stories from them with uncomfortable Spanish. Stories get abbreviated on paper in scribbly writing. Paper gets crinkled up and stuffed into my pockets, then taken out again and unfolded in a little office downtown. The office smells like instant coffee and old books. Scribbly writing becomes double-spaced, Times/New London font with one inch margins. Stories get condensed to fit the little forms. Forms become numbers, numbers become statistics, statistics become colorful graphs. Graphs get pulled out at meetings with judges and police chiefs, pointed at and argued over. Judges and police chiefs pull out their own graphs to point at. And so on and so on.

4.

He can pick me out from a block away.

He's not sure if I'm American but he knows I'm not Mexican. I spot him too, and try to avoid eye contact.

"Bro!"

Damn.

"Bro, you speak English?"

...

"Look I got blasted last night and I don't know what happened. I think those bastards took my wallet. I need to get to Rosarito by tonight. Can you spare some cash for bus fare? You speak English?"

"No."

5.

Fewer migrants have died at the Tijuana crossing point since Gatekeeper because almost no one crosses there any more. They don't bother. Instead the crossing traffic moved further east into the deep desert, where the migrants continue to cross in even greater numbers than before. The death toll has risen by 500% from what it was before Gatekeeper.

But that's not the point.

How can we trust numbers ever again after witnessing how deceiving they can be? The point isn't encoded in percentages or charts. It isn't even buried in those plight-of-the-migrant-worker articles that journalists write when they get back from the border.

6.

A photograph:

Jenny, the 22-year-old American college student, radiantly mediocre-looking after a day of touring around the city with her border studies class. Her designer t-shirt and jeans are a little dusty, her smile a little forced. Beside her is Eduardo, bearded, filthy, devastated, two months out from Michoacan and smiling broadly. They are almost touching, but not quite. Behind them is the old vacant lot and beyond that the border itself.

They say this is where the First World meets the Third. As if the two were old friends that bumped into each other on the street and shook hands, reminisced about old times and walked on. As if the Third World wasn't living in the alleys and prisons of the First World. As if San Diego wasn't edging, building by building, away from the border, while Tijuana inches closer and closer every day.

7.

La Zona Norte, Tijuana:

For a dime you can play an old arcade game with a ten year old dressed like his mariachi father. For a few dollars you can have a one-night stand. For a few more you can have a decent dinner in a little cantina. A fat old barber is passed out in his barbershop chair, his arms splayed out to either side, he's snoring loudly. Two Asian prostitutes keep watch, standing like bodyguards with their arms akimbo. Someone's begging you for money from a pile of newspapers and rags. The world is going about its business at all hours of the night. There're bakeries, pay-by-the-hour hotels, strip clubs. The tourists travel in packs when they come through here, and then brag about it when they make it out alive.

8.

South Hadley, Massachusetts:

The contorted, pleading faces and bodies of migrants adorn the walls of this cozy cultural center at Mt. Holyoke College. The black and white migrants beg for money, huddle with their children, stand symbolically next to the border and get arrested. Inside the circle of photos, students and faculty sip fruit punch and nibble carefully on "Mexican-style" refreshments, which turns out to be jalapeño cheese on wheat-thins.

In one picture, a middle-aged woman in rags holds one hand up to shield her face and with the other pulls her young child in towards her body. She glares past her hand into the camera and past the camera into my eyes like she's looking down the barrel of a gun.

9.

La Avenida Revolución, Tijuana:

Knick-knacks and trinkets. Grinning cartoon Mexicans drinking tequila on white t-shirts on white people. Grinning real Mexicans yelling at everyone who walks by. Pictures on the zebra-painted donkey. Pastel artwork to hang your keys on. Grinning faces of death playing the saxophone. "Come inside my friend! Beautiful pussy! Pussy buffet!" The thump-thump-thump of American techno. Indigenous peasants selling statues of Christ and Spiderman. Fast food. Neon dancing ladies bending over and spreading their neon dancing legs, bending over and spreading their neon dancing legs, again and again until the morning. Cuban cigars. Security forces with automatic weapons and pouty faces. Piñatas shaped like zebras. Another bus from San Ysidro lets off another load of smartly dressed tourists and heads back towards the border...

10.

A video:

The women are well dressed in that carefully exotic flowery look, hair permed, nails done, wrinkles meticulously dispatched beneath several layers of face cream. They regard my cameraman and me with a degree of caution, but seem relieved to speak English and show off what they bought. "You see, Mary and I have this little tradition we like to do: we call it Third World Shopping! We try to go shopping in third world countries. I mean, it's exciting, the bargains are amazing and you can always barter them even lower."

"Look at this handbag I just bought. In San Diego this bag would cost me at least a hundred to a hundred-fifty bucks, right? I got this baby from seventy-five down to forty dollars. Forty! Designer label."

"Last year we went to the Bahamas and Cuba. They had these little Ché and Fidel dolls there that were just precious."

"And next year we're planning a trip to India."

"Well, we'll see..."

11.

Pity.

Is that the best we can do? Is that how far we've come after all these years of trying? Is that what we're left with at the end of each human interest story and photo exhibit?

Roll out the carpet of clichés. Prepare for the stunning finale.

The city of contradiction, which sits on the border between two countries of contradiction inside a whole world of contradiction, which we are either a part of or not. Which we are a part of like it or not. Which we take part in every time we click the shutter, with every dollar we spend and every word we write. Where the First World meets the Third, which is in every country on every continent. The fiction of a line, protected by non-fictional guns and walls. The fiction of standing outside something, protected by dollars and passports, hiding behind metaphors and the play of shadows across a migrant woman's face.

We, the tourists, are the true freaks, the mysteries of nature, the ones-to-watch-out-for. Third World Shopping. The poetry of death. I walked down that hill of dust, away from the circle of migrants sharing mayo and salami sandwiches. I walked through row after row of cars waiting to cross the border, policemen, police dogs and piñata vendors weaving in and out of the traffic. I was the lone cowboy. I was the demon half-breed. A city of contradictions and clichés. A ball of fire. A fucking sunset. I was trying to do something good for the world, and really I was just passing out sandwiches and turning stories into graphs.

History was catching up to me, sweeping up behind me like a phantom ferris wheel, like a hot rush of wind, forcing itself down my throat, into my lungs, my blood. I turned down a side street, walked quickly between dilapidated old shacks with broken windows. Where the First World meets the Third. Where the First World comes to go shopping, have cheap sex and spend college grant money. Where the Third World performs itself night after night in bite-sized vignettes, each with a beginning, middle and end, each safely confined to a stage. A petting zoo. A wax museum. I knew there was something more to do, somewhere to go besides home, something to feel besides sympathy.

Then I stepped on a dead pigeon, watched the crimson pool spread around its little gray body and wiped gut off my tennis shoe. I marched on, ignoring the uneven feeling beneath my feet, closing my eyes and concentrating as hard as I could to break out of the cycle.

46

Francisco Bustos

Madre's right, why you complainin?

You complain and
you got smooth roads
camps and schools
piled with top honors,
you want to scream
while you got steel chairs
and wooden stools
that shine and rent
during prime-time
dreaming us
into voids of senseless laughter.
You got all those eyes
following you along
while you drive
those gleaming wheels
that could almost fly.
Oh, you got everything
and everyone is set
with buttons pressed,
si, como no,
bien guardadito estas
or should I say estamos,
ready to burn, you sing
cause you got courts and medals
from winning races
with trophies a la gold,
got direct-deposits
and four-oh-one-kays
and you got stereos
and there's heads at every corner
talkin nowhere
after battles
of countless circles
trying to touch some peace
some of them lost for good
but you're fine
cause you haven't broken,
plus, you got unlimited cable-all,
cable this, cable that, cable todo man.
So what's the whole big fuss about?

Tu Madre 'sta bien, por que te quejas?

Te quejas y
tienes carreteras lizas
campos y escuelas
montadas con honores altos,
quieres gritar
mientras tienes sillas de fierro
y banquitos de madera
que brillan y se rentan
mientras el prime-time
nos sigue soñando
a vacíos de risas sin rumbo.
 Tienes a todos aquellos ojos
que siguen tu onda
mientras manejas
esas llantas que iluminan
que casi pueden volar.
Uh, tu tienes todo
y todos estan alistados
con botones bien presionados,
si, como no,
bien guardadito estas
oh tal vez debería decir, estamos
listo para quemar, tu cantas
porque tienes cortes y medallas
de carreras ganadoras
con trofeos a la gold,
tienes depósito directo
y four-o-one-kays
y tienes estereos
y hay cabezas en todas las esquinas
hablando hacia ningun lugar
despues de batallas
de círculos interminables
tratando de tocar paz
algunos de ellos perdidos para siempre
pero tu estas bien
porque no has quebrado
y aparte tienes cable sin limite y en todo,
cable esto, cable aquello, cable todo man.
Entonces cual es toda tu bronca pues?

Jensea Storie

Above the Fields

> *Hundreds of thousands of wetbacks*
> *lived in tents or under bridges*
> *eking out a meager diet of greens culled*
> *from ditches on the roadside.*
> —from Sal Si Puedes
> [Get Out if You Can]

I pray to you from a place where hunger
is far deeper than what I've known:
Your home, an endless orchard lit
by faraway suns where goldfinches dress
the stars and moons of your fields.
What do you do day after endless day?
Listen to the fermented prayers
of my toothless father, his back crumbled
like a crucifix abandoned in the Cuyamaca hills?
Lift the tired limbs of my penniless son
who plucks berries down furrows, his green bones
bending? Do you laugh at us when we piss
behind the grower's house? Shrug
your shoulders at borrachos who wake
with tremors only to stagger
like puppets to guzzle more wine.
I can only imagine your voice:
a heat buried beneath rusted trucks, beneath
these fields that peel away our pinched
smiles scattered in the broken clouds
of pesticide fumes dusted
on strawberries stranded on stems.
If I had a door to open, perhaps,
you would enter, telling me everything:
the gleam of clear water on stones
in the infinite fields of your eyes.

Trissy McGhee

This is How You Dance *Danzón*

We went to a bar on Plaza Cecilia, near the *"Bienvenidos a Tijuana"* sign that greets the tourists when they cross the border. The bar was dark and smelled like piss. Anna and I were the only women there except for a tired waitress in a short white skirt and dark hose. She nodded at us when we walked in and I made a mental note to tip her.

Dirk ordered two *caguamas* of Tecate. Someone put some music on the jukebox: Jose Alfredo Jimenez. Anna and Dirk chatted while she squirted lime into her beer. She was asking about his ex-fiancée. They laughed and drank.

I only half listened to them talk. I was watching a man sitting alone at a nearby table. He had on the white cowboy hat I saw so often on men who'd come to T.J. from rural places. Ranch states like Durango, Chihuahua, Sinaloa. The Wyomings and Montanas of Mexico. He sipped his beer slowly, his puffy eyes never leaving the wall in front of him. I couldn't tell if he was listening to the words of the song or not but I imagined he was.

"Why don't you go ask him to dance?" Dirk said.

"Shut up," I laughed and drank my beer.

"Why are you staring at that guy?"

"Just wondering what his story is." I said.

"He's getting drunk on a Friday night, that's his story." Dirk narrowed his eyes and considered me. "So what's your deal? You gonna be a nun or what?"

"What?" I looked at Anna. She rolled her eyes and shrugged.

"We've been in TJ for three months and as far as I can tell you never talk about old boyfriends, never date guys. You a lesbian?"

"I don't think so." I laughed even though I didn't feel like it.

Anna nodded at me. "You just don't date, right?"

"Yeah, kinda." My throat felt tight.

"But you told me you had sex."

"Yeah." I nodded. "Once. Bad sex. I was just getting it over with."

"All first sex is bad sex," Anna said, nodding wisely. "Don't give up on it."

"I'm twenty-eight. I'm running out of time."

"Twenty-eight is pretty young." she shrugged.

"If you want," Dirk leaned forward, "I'll take you in the bathroom and show you what good sex is like." He raised his eyebrows like Groucho Marx

"Piss off," I said. Anna shook her head and laughed.

The waitress came over and we ordered more beer. The man in the hat had left, to make his drunken way home.

"I'm going to start crying if this music doesn't get a little more lively," Dirk said as the waitress set two tall *caguamas* on the table. Anna poured me a glassful. I took a long swig.

A short man with a small wooden box entered the bar. He went slowly from table to table, bowing to each person and muttering in a low voice. One by one the men in the bar shook their heads and turned him away.

"What the hell's that all about?" Dirk asked. Anna turned around to look and I shrugged. Our eyes followed his progress through the bar. I hoped it wasn't some kind of pitiful animal he was selling. I saw that all the time: guys on street corners with dirty white puppies, holding them up to cars for hours and hours. People with tiny caged parrots snapped up out of the jungles of the south to be sold on the border. You could sell anything in Tijuana. I hated the buying and selling of misery. I couldn't stomach it.

The man was getting closer. I could see him muttering furtively with the guys at the table across from us. He kept glancing up at the waitress as if he expected to be kicked out at any second. She ignored him.

"I have got to know what's in that box," Dirk said. The round-faced man said something as he made his way toward us and I was filled with dread. I had to know what was in that box, too

Dirk's eyes glowed darkly when the man shuffled to our table.

"Ask him what it is," Dirk whispered, his hand rubbing his chin.

The man was older than I thought and the box trembled in his soft, wrinkled hands. He approached our table with apprehension on his face, unsure, I supposed, if we spoke any Spanish.

Ah, *Señoritas, Señor,*—he bowed and opened the box just enough for us to see.

For a small fee, he explained in Spanish, the *Señor* can test himself with this machine.

His contraption was some kind of jerry-rigged battery with a crude handle, bare metal, that I assumed was for the customer to grip and hold as long as he could.

"Why the hell would anyone want to do that?" I asked in English.

Para que, Señor? Anna asked the man

To show his strength, he answered, smiling at Dirk. If he wants, the man leaned closer, the Señor can enter a contest against me, to see who can bear the greatest shock.

"What did he say?" Dirk asked. Anna translated quickly.

"Like a bet?" he asked, his eyes glinting. "Ask him how much."

"Don't," I said. "Don't do it, Dirk."

"We're not dragging your corpse through the streets of T.J." Anna shook her head.

Dirk leaned back and looked at us through half-closed cat eyes. Finally he laughed. *"No gracias, Señor,"* he said. The man looked at us coolly and walked to the next table.

Anna and I looked at each other and laughed.

"Jesus," Anna shook her head and took her last swig of beer.

"That's the most Spanish I've ever heard you speak." I told Dirk.

"Ha ha," he slugged his beer.

"That just proves to me how weird men are. It's cross-cultural."

"Do you think that's dangerous?" Anna asked Dirk.

"I don't know, but my balls hurt just thinking about it."

We laughed.

At midnight we finished our beer and walked across the plaza to *La Ballena.*

"This should be interesting," Anna said. "Braulio said it's a prostitute bar."

"Maybe I'll get a date." said Dirk.

"Who's Braulio?" I asked, but Anna didn't hear me. She'd spotted her friends, a table full of young Mexican students. They looked like rock stars: tattoos, shaggy hair, slim leather jackets. We introduced ourselves and squeezed into their booth. They were talking and laughing in quick, slangy Spanish that Dirk and I couldn't follow, but fortunately the guy sitting to my right wanted to practice English. He noticed me looking around.

"See that woman by the bar?"

He nudged me. I looked at her. A woman, a little younger than me, smoking a cigarette and laughing with the bartender. She was wearing a short green skirt and thin stiletto heels. She leaned back on the stool when she exhaled her smoke. "She's a prostitute."

"Oh, yeah?"

She caught me looking and a hot flush crept up my neck. She looked like she could be any young girl from any little *colonia* around here.

"She's cute," Dirk said. "Dude, can I .." he motioned to the Faro filterless cigarettes on the table.

"*Claro*." He offered a cigarette to Dirk and then to me. I shook my head. "This might be a stupid question, um...Alberto, was it?" He nodded, lighting his cigarette. "Is it legal in Mexico? Prostitution?"

"Only in the Zona Rosa. Coahuila. We are very close by now. If you walk that way," he pointed north, "along *Revolucion* you will reach 2nd Avenue, Coahuila. All that area is the Red-Light district. You will see there many women on the street, waiting in doorways. These are the prostitutes."

"That's a rough job," I said. But Dirk was asking Alberto about gambling at the Jai Alai. I looked back at the bar but the young woman was gone. Break over.

I was drunk. Nicely and happily drunk, all glow and no hard edges. More beers appeared in front of us and we drank. Someone put a song on the jukebox and everyone in the booth got up to dance. I didn't notice when a second song played or even a third but the fourth song was slow and heavy. People started to sit back down and I wanted to sit as well but a tall boy blocked my way.

I'd met him earlier but I couldn't remember his name. Guillermo, maybe. He said something to me in Spanish and I said "*Mande?*" and tipped forward until my nose nearly touched his shirt. We both laughed.

In perfect English he said, "This song is called a Danzón. Have you heard of it?"

I shook my head and felt a giggle surfacing inside of me. Guillermo took my hands before I even knew what he was doing.

"This is how to dance Danzón."

He steered me slowly, holding me as if for a waltz. "The movement is like a box, like a square. No."

He held his hands up for a moment to make a box. All I could think was how I wanted him to let me sit back down. But my feet moved with a drunken looseness, they followed his lead before my mind knew what they were doing. He kept telling me to slow down, to feel the heavy cadence of the music. "*Es como una contradanza*—ballroom dancing. But tropical too."

"Is this a Mexican dance?" I was nervous, trying not to stare at my feet. I hoped my hands weren't clammy.

He shook his head. "It has everything in it: Europe, Africa,

Latin America." He nodded at my feet. "Good, like that."

We were the only ones dancing but everyone in the booth was watching us and smiling. My face was hot.

I closed my eyes and let the tall boy lead me. Slow quick quick. Slow quick quick. The music began to take over and I relaxed a little. I hadn't felt this way in a long time. Loose. All my joints stopped stuttering and my muscles began to flow. As long as I didn't look around I knew I'd be OK. I half-smiled, eyes closed, and kept going.

His arm slid down my back. I tasted a flash of desire in my mouth, sharp and surprising. I liked the feel of a body against mine, stirred by music, moving slowly. I thought: *This is what connection is like. This is what people do.*

We shuffled on. I bit my lip, afraid I was going to laugh.

"It's a beautiful dance," I said. "It feels like—desire."

As soon as I said it I felt stupid. I didn't meet his eyes. I was still half hoping he'd let me go sit down. The other half didn't know what it was hoping for.

He didn't smile, just kept moving me across the floor in front of the jukebox. We moved heavily through the music. I could feel the warmth of his body: hands, arms, hips pressed to mine. I turned my head drunkenly to look for the prostitute. Desire was the game she dealt in every day. I wanted to talk to her about that, to understand how it all worked.

"There's only one place to experience the Danzón," Guillermo said, bending close to my head.

I didn't know what he meant, but I nodded and looked around at the dark bar full of cigarette smoke and people whose stories I wanted to hear. Everyone a little drunk, a little lonely. Everyone watching the skinny *fresa* teach the *gavacha* to dance. The shift of hips, the slow shuffle. Watching as I learned to slow everything down, because Danzón is all ache.

"Do you feel it?" he said.

I nodded. I felt it.

School

Photo by Hendrix Knowells

Hector Martinez
Como Un Corrido
para T. McGhee

Border town. A boy, with a grown man's
concern for bringing home food, or saving

his feet, the blistered toes and bulging foot
knuckles, from shoes quickly outgrown. At ten

he still can't read, or even write his name.
But after work—trades wooden broom for

pencil; labors in the learning of words.
Naranja, zapatos, cobija—any poor boy's

dreams—letters fat with error, he searches
his teacher's green eyes. To him, they are

a glimpse beyond the border, the rolling
hills of the other side. Method: hand over

hand, she guides, the R, the a, the m, and
still, he fades into the empty table.

"Maybe"—he thinks— "I'm dumb"—he leaves
But later—rhythm— the way song—harmony—

enters the mind—melody—on a
sidewalk—Ramon—he writes: Ramon—

como un corrido—Ramon—
His name—Ramon—a song.

Photo by Rachel Jones 2005

McMansion on the Hill:
In Chula Vista, explosive growth has pushed the median
price of a new home from $339,000 in 2002 to $415,000
in 2005. Stressed for success, suburbanites take comfort
in the architecture of reassurance.

Mark Dery

Loving the Alien: Or, How I Learned to Stop Worrying and Become Californian

Born in Boston and raised in New England until I was five, I felt like Robinson Crusoe on Mars when we moved to San Diego. Marooned in a suburban development, I rode my Sting-Ray down gridded streets, past lookalike tract homes. If I squinted hard, I could almost imagine I was one of the crabgrass frontiersmen in Ray Bradbury's *Martian Chronicles* (1950), homesteading in some extraterrestrial Levittown. To someone from "back East," the climate was alien: It never snowed, it rarely rained, and on the hottest days the sun seemed as if it was about to go nova.

"Rocket Summer," the prose poem that opens *The Martian Chronicles*, is an Atom Age folk tale about every immigrant's first encounter with the surreality of Southern California weather, a drama reenacted by generations of new arrivals. Born in Waukegan, Illinois, Bradbury moved with his family to Los Angeles in 1934. Like so many transplants, he put down mental roots and grew up to find himself a member of that exotic species, *Homo californius*. The transformation of uprooted easterner into honorary native is a Californian rite of passage, wryly noted by Raymond Chandler in his screenplay for *Double Indemnity* (1944). "Where did you pick up this tea drinking?," Walter Neff (Fred MacMurray) asks Phyllis Dietrichson (Barbara Stanwyck). "You're not English, are you?"

Phyllis: No. Californian. Born right here in Los Angeles.
Walter: They say native Californians all come from Iowa.

In "The Million-Year Picnic," the story that ends *The Martian Chronicles*, Bradbury translates the eastern immigrant's shock of recognition at the bleached-blond, gold-skinned alien staring back from the mirror into the Martian vernacular. Boating past dead cities, alien boneyards "drowsing in a hot silence of summer," a family of Midwesterners debarks to prowl the Martian metropolis they've chosen for their new home. When one of the kids asks where all the Martians have gone, Dad points down, into the dark waters of a canal.

Photo by Rachel Jones 2005

Extraterrestrial Levittown:
Chula Vista sprawls eastward.

> The Martians were there—in the canal—reflected in
> the water. Timothy and Michael and Robert and
> Mom and Dad.
> The Martians stared back up at them for a long, long
> silent time from the rippling water...

As Mike Davis points out in *City of Quartz, The Martian Chronicles* "revolves around contradictions between the Turnerian, 'westering' quest for new frontiers and poignant nostalgia for smalltown America." Writing in L.A., the most *Blade Runner* of all American cities, Bradbury has always looked homeward, nurturing a conservative yearning for the Waukegan of the 1920s (reimagined in his fiction as the idyllic, unchanging Greentown, Illinois) even as he dreams pulp dreams of space colonization and better living through social engineering.

This tension reverberates throughout *The Martian Chronicles*, where Rockwellian renderings of turn-of-the-century, smalltown America are set, incongruously, against a Martian backdrop. "It was as if, in many ways, a great earthquake had shaken loose the roots and cellars of an Iowa town, and then, in an instant, a whirlwind twister of Oz-like proportions had carried the entire town off to Mars and set it down without a bump," he writes, in "February 2003: Interim."

The push-pull between Bradbury's nostalgia for a sentimentalized Midwestern past and his Californian faith in utopian experiments is paralleled in the work of another pop mythmaker and Midwestern transplant: Walt Disney. In the Disneyland of my youth, Bradbury-esque fantasies were writ large in Tomorrowland's Adventure Thru Inner Space Presented by Monsanto, the McDonnell Douglas Flight to the Moon, and the General Electric Carousel of Progress—monuments to military-industrial progress, erected by the smiling corporate dictator whose Monorails and PeopleMovers always ran on time. (Bradbury, a fervent Disney fan, once exhorted the imagineer to run for mayor of L.A., on the assumption that "he was the only man with enough technological imagination to rationalize the sprawling mess the megalopolis had become," notes Richard Schickel, in *The Disney Version*.)

Yet Tomorrowland is only a monorail ride away from Main Street, U.S.A., the quaint, 5/8 scale recreation of 1890s America that welcomes visitors to the Happiest Place on Earth. In her biography of her father, Diane Disney Miller interprets Main Street, with its horse-drawn streetcars and barbershop quartet, as Disney's valentine to the fondly remembered Marceline, Missouri of his youth. To Schickel, the psychobiographical subtext is "too perfect—the strangers forced to recapitulate Disney's formative experience before being allowed to visit his fancies and fantasies in the other areas of the Magic Kingdom." True, but Disney's control-freak impulses are in the service, here, of a wish-fulfillment fantasy designed for white, middle-class Midwesterners who, like Disney, dream of time-traveling back to the hometowns they left behind.

When Disney and Bradbury moved to California, in 1924 and '34 respectively, such longings were widespread. In his 1946 study, *Southern California: An Island on the Land*, the historian Carey McWilliams confirms Walter Neff's folk wisdom that native-born Californians have always constituted a minority in the state, and that most of the immigrants who flooded Southern California between 1900 and 1930 were, in fact, from Iowa. (Many of the others were from Illinois, like Bradbury and his family, or from Ohio, like the townspeople pointing their rockets Mars-ward in "Rocket Summer.")

Homesickness shadowed the new lives of many who came to the Golden State. Transposing this "great illness" to Mars, Bradbury re-imagines it as "The Loneliness," the inner void that expands as his colonists hurtle into space, "because when you saw your hometown dwindle the size of your fist and then lemon-size and then pin-size and vanish in the fire-wake, you felt you had never been born, there was no town, you were nowhere, with space all around, nothing familiar, only other strange men. And when the state of Illinois, Iowa, Missouri, or Montana vanished into cloud seas...then you were alone, wandering in the meadows of space, on your way to a place you couldn't imagine."

In Los Angeles, a nowhere with space all around and nothing familiar, immigrants invoked the lost worlds of Waukegan, Marceline, and places further east through oxymoronic architecture designed to make them feel at home. An Iowan quoted by McWilliams tells of the homes built by his fellow transplants, each with an Iowa-style porch for neighborly evenings spent porch-sitting. As they soon discovered, there's precious little porch-sitting in Southern California, where "night followed day as suddenly as the dropping of a curtain, without a romantic twilight," and "the evenings, even in summer, were so cold that they would have to muffle themselves in their buffalo overcoats." New England immigrants memorialized their nostalgia, too, in homes "with high steep roofs to shed the snow that did not fall, with dark interiors that contrasted nightmarishly with the bright out-of-doors, and with deep cellars built for needless furnaces." Future Californians would look back on these insistently, absurdly out-of-place dwellings with the affectionate condescension of the Martians in Bradbury's "Dark They Were, and Golden Eyed." Casting a bemused eye on an abandoned Earth settlement, one remarks, "Such odd, ridiculous houses the Earth people built." To which his wife replies, "They didn't know any better."

As the journalist Garet Garrett said of the metamorphosis of Midwesterner into Martian, "The mind is first adjusted, then the conscious feelings; but for a long time—for the rest of the immigrant's life, perhaps—there will be in the cells a memory of home that was elsewhere."

In the late 19th century, rootless newcomers eager to bond with others from their home states formed social clubs called "state societies," now largely extinct. Society ranks swelled with lonely Midwesterners, newly arrived in this alien place. In the '20s, notes McWilliams, an Iowa Society picnic in Long Beach drew 150,000 Iowans. Inevitably, however, the day came when Iowans looked at themselves in the mirror and saw L.A.-liens looking back. "With the passing of so many first-generation immigrants," writes McWilliams, "the state societies have begun to decline..." He quotes a wistful old Iowan: "If the boys and girls were born in Iowa, and remembered it, then they didn't mind coming along with their parents to the picnic, but Iowa means nothing to the California-born grandchildren. You can't get these native-born Californians to a state-society meeting." The children of the Earthlings' children are sun-bronzed aliens "with gold coin eyes," Martian by birth.

The critic Reyner Banham embroidered this thread in *Los Angeles: The Architecture of Four Ecologies:*

> If Los Angeles is not a monolithic Protestant moral tyranny—and it notoriously is not!—it is because the Midwestern agrarian culture underwent a profound transformation as it hit the coast, a sun-change that pervades moral postures, political attitudes, ethnic groupings, and individual psychologies. This change has often been observed, and usually with bafflement, yet one observer has bypassed the bafflement and gone straight to an allegory of Californiation that seems to hold good from generation to generation —Ray Bradbury in the most fundamental of his Martian stories, "Dark They Were

And Golden Eyed," where the earth family are sub-
tly transformed, even against their wills, into tall,
bronzed, gold-eyed Martians who abandon their
neat Terran cities and the earthly cares and duty
they symbolize, and run free in the mountains.

San Diego is no moral tyranny, either, but neither is it a
Brechtian Mahagonny like L.A. As Banham points out, a "Martian
transformation" was forced on Midwesterners who migrated to
Los Angeles by virtue of the fact that their rural or smalltown
ways of life vaporized on contact with the local economy and soci-
ety. Family farming, the occupation into which many Midwestern
immigrants had been born, was largely unknown in Southern
California, where agriculture was big business, dominated by
large-scale operations.

As well, there was Hollywood's pervasive, erosive influence on
bible-belt morality and the homely values of heartland immi-
grants. According to Banham:

Hollywood brought to Los Angeles an unprecedent-
ed and unrepeatable population of genius, neuro-
sis, skill, charlatanry, beauty, vice, talent, and
plain old eccentricity, and it brought that popula-
tion in little over two decades... So Hollywood was
also the end of innocence and provincialism—the
movies found Los Angeles a diffuse fruit-growing
super-village of some eight hundred thousand
souls, and handed it over to the infant television
industry in 1950 a world metropolis of over four
million.

(By contrast, the city of San Diego's population at that time
was 333,865. The county total was 556,808.) San Diego has no
Hollywood to corrupt its family values. On the contrary: the mili-
tary—the major underwriter of the local economy since 1919,
when the Navy chose the city as home base for the Pacific Fleet—
has added steel reinforcement to the moral infrastructure of the
city's God-fearing, law-abiding Midwestern immigrants and con-
servative retirees. "Conservatism dominated San Diego's political
thinking," Richard F. Pourade confirms, in *The History of San
Diego*. "There was a heavy concentration of military personnel,
both active and retired, as well as many pensioners from the
Midwest. Conservative ideology was brought to bear on the voters
by the quiet yet persuasive James S. Copley, through his *San*

Diego Union." (As the editors of the *San Diego Historical Society* website note, Copley's "unabashedly conservative, Republican, and pro-American" politics continue to "have a deep influence on the voting populace of San Diego" even after his death, by virtue of his boosterish, reflexively pro-business newspaper—the only major daily in town.) In 1960, when John F. Kennedy captured the White House, San Diego County cast a majority vote for Nixon. In 1964, when President Lyndon Johnson ran for re-election, winning in a national landslide, San Diego was solidly behind Republican Senator Barry Goldwater.

Born in Boston but raised, from age six on, in Southern California, I thought of myself as a stranger in a strange land—a dark-haired E.T. in a blond world, a pale-skinned bookworm who burned and peeled but never tanned. My home planet was the East Coast, mythologized in my parents' tall tales as a place of frozen locks, cars that wouldn't start, endless snowstorms, and even more endless shoveling. East Coast partisans manage to get misty-eyed about white Christmases and the turning of the leaves, but only a masochist could truly love a region whose weather alternates between subzero and subtropical. In the winter, a drive to the corner store turns into a Shackleton expedition, complete with gale-force winds. In the summer, a miasma of sour sweat and foul humor hangs over cities such as New York, wrapping everything in a wet blanket. But at least the East Coast has culture, the reasoning goes.

In 1965, we migrated westward in that mid-sixties hybrid of Conestoga wagon and personal rocketship, the Volkswagen van, our worldly goods lashed to the rooftop rack. For my stepdad, a machinist, California dangled the hope of a high-paying job in the booming aeronautics and aerospace industries. On a deeper level, he was seduced by the libertarian promise that had drawn generations of easterners yearning to be free of New England's puritan prudery, its tight-lipped Yankee reserve, its pinched provincialism. In Jean-Paul Dery's version of our family's founding myth, "Things were fresh and new in California, not stinted and narrow as they were in tiny cramped New England," as he recalled, in a recent e-mail interview. "I was going to go to a land where I would never have to shovel snow again, or go without a beer because the liquor stores (they call them package stores back there in Connecticut [because] they are so tight-assed they won't say 'liquor') closed at noon on Saturday and did not open again till Monday. I felt Californians were open-minded, and friendly to everybody."

When we arrived in San Diego, Jean-Paul ("J.P." to his

friends) was delighted to discover that utopia had lived up to its advertising campaign: "California had things that Connecticut would not get for years," he noted, chief among them a climate that was pure paradise, followed closely by beer on Sundays. Topless dancers and nude beaches left no doubt that we were "far from the puritan morés of the New Englanders." In our interview, he rhapsodized, "Out here it was Freedom city and let it all hang out. New, racy, exciting, and open-ended, not confining and controlling like the way I used to feel in New England." For Californians, freedom and freeways are synonymous, and J.P. followed suit, embracing the swooping, multi-lane roads as proof of personal liberty: "No tolls on the highways—what a concept! Where I came from, you couldn't drive five miles without hitting a toll booth."

My mom was less sanguine about the New World. A New England Yankee, she was torn between post-traumatic memories of Boston blizzards and a Brahmin's disdain for San Diego's middlebrow attempts at culture, from the symphony's Lawrence Welk repertoire of "pops" and light classics to the Museum of Art's determinedly inoffensive, retiree-friendly fare. San Diego *culture*?! Quel oxymoron! It is to laugh! One might as well ask: Is there life on Mars?

Alienation was my birthright, the inevitable by-product of a bicoastal disorder that split my personality down the middle. Like my mom, I sneered at San Diego's whoa-dude vacuity, wearing what Robert Lowell called "Massachusetts' low-tide dolor" as a badge of honor in the land of surfers and Smiley Faces. The San Diego religion seemed to be a Stepfordian take on Zen Buddhism's "empty mind," a hybrid of sun worship and the cosmic mellowness of *The Big Lebowski's* Dude.

At the same time, I followed my stepdad, wading hip-deep into California culture, high on the pop flotsam and manmade marvels all around me: lowriders, dune buggies, vans with bubble windows and airbrushed sunsets; futuristic freeways whose swooping flyovers made me feel as if the family wagon was engaging warp drive; Googie styling that turned drive-ins and drive-throughs into Jetsonian spaceports; Ed "Big Daddy" Roth dragster models from Revell; "Odd Rods" kustom kar trading cards; head shops that sold body oils, bootlegs, black-light posters, mentholated "cokesnuff"; and the taco stand, late-night Lourdes of stumbling-drunk gringos.

Nature, too, was worlds away from the East Coast, emblematized in my mind by my maternal grandparents' Cape Cod town, a fog-haunted, Melvillean place of cranberry bogs and marshy beaches, weathered cottages and lobster traps. If New England's miniaturist landscapes were Kodak-moment fodder—autumn leaves and whipped-cream snowdrifts—San Diego nature was big-screen, Sensurround stuff. La Jolla's surreal sandstone bluffs looked like a collaboration between Yves Tanguy and Dr. Seuss. The blasted beauty of the Anza-Borrego desert was at once primordial and post-apocalyptic. And the almighty Pacific, with its majestic green billows, made a mockery of those pathetic knee-slappers East Coasters call waves.

On the East Coast, in a city such as New York, culture was nature. I'll never forget my first subway trip to Coney Island, on one of those sweltering summer days when the air is so humid it's viscous. Reeling out of a packed cattle car, onto the burning sands, I took in a scene that, for a San Diegan, was positively Boschian: bodies, bodies everywhere, and not an inch of sand to spare. A tangle of sweaty flesh extending to the water's edge—flabby, skinny, unconvincingly bronzed or white as a frog's belly. People, people, as far as the eye could see, radios blaring, voices braying, their blankets so close they literally overlapped. The water was as crowded as a municipal pool, and about as foul; the sand was the world's biggest ashtray, bristling with stubbed-out cigarettes. I thought, dizzily, of San Diego's Torrey Pines beach, where a few blocks' hike could win you a cove all your own, and sole deed and title to the limitless ocean around it. Where's Soylent Green when you need it?

In Dery family lore, New Yorkers were the most alien of Easterners—pasty creatures who lay on the beach but never ventured into the water. Alarmingly, many of them actually *smoked*, not yet a capital crime in the permissive '70s, but a *serious* lapse of rectitude, nonetheless. From the asthmatics, rheumatics, and wealthy hypochondriacs who flocked to the city's sanitariums in the 1900s to the joggers and apostles of nutrition guru (and California immigrant) Adelle Davis in the 1970s, San Diegans have long taken healthful living (or, at least, the surgically enhanced appearance of it) as seriously as the dietary prohibitions in Leviticus.

Not only were New Yorkers unapologetically unhealthy, but they were uncouth, to boot, mangling SoCal's Spanish place names in the *dese-and-demspeak* of old gangster movies. Their clothes were loud, too—tacky, synthetic-fiber get-ups better suited to a blackjack table in Atlantic City than to laid-back San Diego, where OP surfware and puka shells, *guayaberas* and Harachi sandals were the standard-issue uniform, accessorized with mirrored sunglasses. Even their cars were vulgar: road-hog-

Photo by Rachel Jones 2005

Edge of Empire:
In one of Chula Vista's Eastlake developments, a
Rottweiler stands guard against illegal aliens.

ging Cadillacs that looked like throwbacks to the Land That Time Forgot, when bada-bing hustlers in sharkskin suits and pinky rings ruled the world.

It never occurred to me, at the time, that a racist subtext lurked beneath many of these stereotypes. San Diego is a city whose prevailing attitudes have been shaped, for most of its modern history, by conservative whites: smalltown Midwesterners, bible-belt Southerners, senior citizens enjoying their golden years in San Diego's law-abiding paradise, and, as noted earlier, retired and active-duty military personnel. Cold-war conservatism exacerbated the backwoods bigotry of the rural and smalltown whites who made up much of the city's immigrant stock.

Little surprise, then, that the city had a disproportionately small population of blacks and Mexican-Americans, compared to other large cities. Minorities didn't need a sign posted at city limits, reading "no blacks or Mexicans need apply," to get the message. When my family moved to Chula Vista, in 1966, San Diego was the 16th largest city in the United States, with a population of nearly 640,000. Yet, as of 1960, Mexican-Americans constituted only six-and-six-tenths percent of San Diego's population, with blacks making up a roughly equal percentage of the total. The handful of Mexican-Americans in my high school, Hilltop High, were the light-skinned fortunate sons and daughters of Tijuana's ruling class, raised in Chula Vista's toniest neighborhoods. Out of a student body of 2,000, there were maybe three blacks.

The incredible whiteness of being San Diegan wasn't a coincidence. The city rolled out its unwelcome mat for people of color in the form of economic and social discrimination. Politicians, developers, and real-estate barons used redlining to cordon off blacks, Mexicans, and low-income whites (codeword: white trash), quarantining them in the city's less desirable neighborhoods, such as Logan Heights and Golden Hill. "Protection against adverse influences is obtained by the existence and enforcement of proper zoning regulations and appropriate deed restrictions," informed the August 1, 1935 edition of the *FHA Underwriting Manual*. The *Manual* helpfully defined "adverse influences" as the "infiltration of inharmonious racial or nationality groups" (along with "the presence of smoke, odors, fog, etc."). In the '30s, when eugenics was a respected science and the specter of Spenglerian racial decline haunted White America, the de-facto segregation of redlining protected "respectable" San Diegans from the degenerate underclasses. As late as 1965, San Diego was still "one of the most segregated areas in the country," according to a Fair Employment Practices Commission cited by Jim Miller in *Under the Perfect Sun: The San Diego Tourists Never See.*

Leaving San Diego for New York City, as I did after college, was like emigrating to Mars. Racially and ethnically diverse, delirious New York (to borrow the architect Rem Koolhaas's felicitous phrase) is brash and brutal yet urbane, European in its sophistication but exuberantly American in its appetite for cheap thrills and lurid sensation, its Weegee-esque embrace of the naked city: Lower East Side kids playing in gushing hydrants, murder victims faceplanted on the pavement, rubbernecking crowds, stumbling drunks, grotesques, arabesques, a dwarf in diapers on New Year's Eve. Where San Diego is hidebound, ingrown, New York is omnivorously inclusive—the proverbial "mongrel metropolis." San Diego's vision of the City Beautiful is, in a word, Disneyland: a microbe- and minority-free theme park, underwritten by military-industrial contractors. New York's idea of a syncopated city is Times Square: the devil's playground (before Disney and Giuliani sterilized it), with its porn shops, pentecostal preachers, girls in glass booths, three-card monte dealers, and clip joints selling nunchuks and throwing stars and "genuine" jade tchotchkes. San Diego, in Gore Vidal's memorable epithet, is the "Vatican of the John Birch Society." New York, in the words of Chula Vista homeboy (and, briefly, New York resident) Tom Waits, is "like a ship full of rats, and the water's on fire."

Now, two decades after moving to New York, I think of it as my home planet. Every year or two, I fly west to visit my sister, who lives in Eastlake, on the frontlines of suburban Chula Vista's assault on what used to be canyon country. The McMansions in her master-planned community quote Old-World vernacular and vintage American styles from the developer's pattern book, some of which would look right at home on Disney's Main Street or in the 1926 Illinois town in The Martian Chronicles: "Further up on the green stood a tall brown Victorian house, quiet in the sunlight, all covered with scrolls and rococo, its windows made of blue and pink and yellow and green colored glass..." The names of other developments, posted on a shiny sign—Chambord, Old Creek, Alexandria, Fairhaven—trumpet a parvenu craving for the weight of European history, antebellum elegance, a manor-born assurance about one's place in the social order. Chambord features Maison, Provence, Chateau, and Versailles models; Fairhaven offers Oxford, Essex, Chelsea, and Windsor styles. Even the nearby golf club is named "Auld Course," the Scots dialect summoning visions of gentry in knickers, selecting just the right iron for that treacherous bunker while their caddies look on worshipfully.

Photo by Rachel Jones 2005

Nueva Frontera:
Barbed wire marks the end of San Diego's South County
sprawl. For now.

There's nothing Auld about the club, or any of these develop-ments, but nothing salves the sting of class envy like a name mossy with European history, perfumed by old money. Propelled by "class flight," middle-class and upper middle-class Chula Vistans like my sister and her family are pointing their personal rockets eastward, abandoning the city's increasingly low-income, relatively high-crime downtown neighborhoods for upscale space colonies in what used to be canyon country—an eastward expan-sion halted, for the moment, by San Miguel Mountain. As recent-ly as 1998, my sister recalled, in an e-mail interview, "new hous-es in CV...[were] more affordable. [...] As time progressed, older parts of CV became influxed [sic] with more crimes and the work-ing middle are trying to move up the economic ladder by estab-lishing developments in suburbs outside, but in close proximity to, the city. So, to put it in plain English, we are all living beyond our means: driving our SUVs that get six-to-17 mpg (eight people on our street now own [Hummers]), buying homes large enough for your entire extended family to live with you, trying to outdo the Joneses next door in every aspect—house decor, clothes, cars, and pushing your kids to their limits with education and extracurricular activities."

Sometimes, when I'm visiting, I do something only a New Yorker would do, something a Southern Californian would find deeply suspicious: I go for a walk. Strolling the deserted streets (so un-New York!) of my sister's development, I look for signs of life—little gestures of dissent, or eccentricity, even. I've never seen any, which is hardly surprising, given that, on my sister's street alone, there are six police officers, one retired cop, two firefight-ers, one retired firefighter, six military personnel, and one retired serviceperson, by my sister's count. If there are any Democrats in the 'hood, they're keeping their politically incorrect thoughts to themselves.

As I walk, I feel eyes on my back, from behind the drawn blinds, and wonder if I'm inviting the suspicions of the Neighborhood Watch. Maybe I'll be arrested, like the protagonist of "The Pedestrian," Bradbury's slyly mocking tale of a man taken away, in 2052, for the crime of walking his neighborhood streets. Though it's unnamed, his city can only be L.A.: "The street was silent and long and empty, with only his shadow moving like the shadow of a hawk in mid-country."

True to my sister's words, an SUV hulks in nearly every drive-way, sporting the mandatory yellow-ribbon decal or "Support Our Troops" bumper sticker or sometimes both. Patriotic bunting fringes the balcony of one house; on another, a placard over the door reads, "God Bless Our Home." According to my sister, the woman who lives there cast her vote for George W. Bush because of his opposition to abortion, stem-cell research, and gay marriage. She knows, in her heart, that Darwinian theory is a rotting heap of secular-humanist falsehoods. She believes she may live to see the Rapture, when time shall be no more.

I make my way down the eerily empty streets, shadowless in the apocalyptic sun.

I am the man who fell to Earth.

marion cloete

freedom fighters fall to love
(from a storefront in North Park)

vague the
time before you
every thing and one touched barely
in story and dream

demideath the
fear before. we unpaired
ungathered at the ark.

absence of
prophecy the
hours toward descent. palm lines
at once tangled together

disbelief the
face of my face
coy my insh'allations
shy my incantations

          hopes how
          hopes recite hopes
          as tortured state maps we secede. eyes
          fluent in refuge

l.g.kanga

exile

             make them scatter place in soil (in oceans)

in such ways that make them scatter when   breezes blew make them spread and
  scatter dislodged amongst weeds   oceans so when light winds blue like
oceans would take them off course   (of course) carrying and setting
them on concrete grounds (on   oceans) in concrete jungles (in
oceans) set in asphalt (in   oceans) in such ways
  and water and   make them scatter place in soil in   oceans would only
  bind make the   such ways that make them scatter   living harder so
frozen seeds   when breezes blew make them   float (with
oceans)   spread and scatter dislodged in   crystal
lining   concrete   their
shells (their   oceans)
  somewhere   underneath all
that is (ocean) life   uncontainable in earth
in seeds (in oceans) and   they will grow (in oceans)
  accustomed to the glazed   ground will ebb and flow (like
oceans) wax like moons (like
    oceans) wane   like moons (like oceans)

Remembrance of Things Past

Photo by Jennifer Cost

MEMORY AND ASH

Matthew Bokovoy
Ghosts of the San Diego Rialto

Every Thursday, Friday, and Saturday night, crowds of college students, underage revelers, urbane wannabees, and white suburban gangsters cruise the streets of lower Broadway in downtown San Diego. They make their way west of 7th Avenue down south into the Gaslamp Quarter, the city's answer to New Orleans' Bourbon Street. The crowds that frequent San Diego's downtown share enthusiasm for an exciting evening on the town after a week committed entirely to work. However, one has to wonder if all the slickness, bright lights, and consumer dreariness of the bars and clubs will wear off one day. Unlike the street-level gravity that absorbs tourists who view the historic structures of New Orleans once they leave Bourbon Street, the Broadway and Gaslamp Quarter historic districts serve as mere decoration for the distraction offered by chain retailers, gaudy bistros, frat bars and sorority sister clubs, and MTV-like street life. For locals and tourists alike, there is simply little of historic interest beyond the consumer pageant that is now downtown San Diego.

With a mood reminiscent of a perpetual spring break, the new San Diego signals the revitalization of downtown after 50 years of unlimited suburban land development. With the completion of Petco Park, John Moores' $453.4 million extortion scheme to deliver a spanking, new downtown baseball stadium to his Padres, hefty returns roll-in as the dreams of former mayor Pete Wilson and San Diego's downtown, old money are realized. The coffers of the bars and clubs, restaurants, real estate developers, and city tax-base flourish as well. With the backdrop of history only 80 to 100 years old, Broadway and the Gaslamp district are commuter fun zones for the newly entitled: relatively empty and business-like during the day; choked full at happy hour and beyond to last call.

Will it last? Perhaps, but maybe the restaurant and entertainment zones of Hillcrest, Middletown, North Park, or Mission Hills will lure the revelers away. With more attention to history that is actually local, these areas will seal the fate of Broadway and the Gaslamp district in the near future. Downtown San Diego's revitalization differs little from other efforts across the country: it is the site for global consumer and real estate capitalism. Over the years that I lived in San Diego (1976-1999), I saw the center city transformed from a ghost town for homeless Vietnam veterans, the mentally ill (50% of vets), and the working poor to a shining exemplar of urban gentrification. The old "sailor town" I knew as a teenager lives only in memory. Downtown had its theaters, libraries, art galleries, and symphony hall that shared an urban environment rife with funky street life, SRO hotels, check-cashing places, modest department stores, go-go bars, book stores, cafeterias, liquor stores, massage parlors, and porn movie houses. San Diego used to be a real city. The heart of this glorious San Diego Rialto used to be Horton Plaza until the suburban-type mall at that site was completed in 1987 defended and turned inward from the fabric of the city. In only twenty years, downtown has become an "upscale" leisure zone of luxury apartment blocks with little housing for the working poor.

San Diego joins other cities in urban gentrification to erase the diverse social networks of urban living, such as San Francisco, Los Angeles, Chicago, Albuquerque, San Antonio, New Orleans, New York, Philadelphia, and Washington, D.C. Gentrification is the velvet glove of class warfare. Public policy formulated to redeem downtown San Diego has not been able to integrate the older constituents, who depend upon center city with new economic and cultural enterprises. Shouldn't this redevelopment benefit the broader public that calls downtown its home, since municipal bonds, public tax subsidies, and public policy shape the new urban environment? With development in eastern San Diego County at capacity, downtown real estate becomes valuable once again. With real estate interests historically serving as the private government of the city, the public interest has been subsumed to private profit.

The diverse social networks of downtown San Diego are the casualties of progress, like every major American metropolis today. Through the efforts of the Centre City Development Corporation (CCDC), charged with public/private urban redevelopment since 1975, much of sailor town and its citizens have been cleansed through the exerted pressure of the private sector. By the 1980s and 1990s, the variety of businesses and people that had fully sustained downtown San Diego since 1900 were defined as "criminal" and a "nuisance" during the latest landgrab. Similar to so many other American cities, the homeless, the working poor, and the Rialto economy held downtown San Diego "hostage." It is without question that this older sailor town economy had at least anchored the tax-base of center city during its most trying times, from the 1950s to the 1980s. All American cities depended upon the economy of the marginal during this era as federal housing policies pushed new development to cheaper suburban lands after World War II. However, San Diego's new cheerleaders of progress, with their pet city councils, will never acknowledge the favor. Once the critical lifeblood of a vital, although poor, downtown, the current urban renaissance has been built upon the ashes of SRO hotels, homeless shelters, and working class economic and entertainment institutions. Perhaps it is built upon more. Recent investigations show that the city's pension fund suffers a $1.15 billion deficit with possible accounting fraud. The city manager and council are under SEC and grand jury investigation. As of this writing, no city official can explain where all the money went. Of course, we can guess by all the recent downtown development. If historic preservation has been the organizing principle for downtown revitalization, private interests have piggy backed on the city's history to great profit to erase the vital social networks of San Diego.

Until the late twentieth century, the history of San Diego's development always catered to a variety of social classes, and people of vastly different cultural heritage and racial ancestry. Indeed, one might say that the founding of San Diego in 1769, like Los Angeles to the north, was christened with the mixed racial origins that are the hallmark of cultural fusion in the southwestern borderlands. San Diego has never had the equivalent of a Carey McWilliams to document its diverse origins. But Harry Crosby reveals that the Serra Expedition of 1769 brought *españoles, mestizos,* color *quebrados, mulatos,* and *indios* to the frontier of northern New Spain to settle Alta California.* In the first fifty-two years of the new settlement, the mission, presidio, and pueblo community emerged as a racially-mixed society engaged in agriculture, cattle raising, and illicit trade with British, American, and French merchant vessels. During the Mexican era after 1822, Old Town San Diego became the center of commerce, politics, and trade, but remained a territorial outpost of southern North America. As the pueblo attended to its daily activities around the plaza, there were Indians, Mexicans, and Anglos engaged in a profitable hide and tallow trade with New England merchants. Richard Henry Dana and other Euro-American travelers in the early nineteenth century noted significant populations of Hawaiians (known as Kanakas), desiccated Anglo adventurers, and Christian and gentile Indians who worked on the ranches, ships, and wharfs

---

* This caste/race system noted *Españoles* were "pure-blooded Spanish"; *mestizos* were Indian and Spanish; color *quebrados* were "broken color," Spanish-Indian with dark skin; *mulatos* were Indian and Spanish, with a trace of African ancestry; and *indios* were "pure-blooded Indians."

engaged in trans-Pacific and Atlantic trade. With powerful Creole sons and their wards closely bound together, town development relied, historically, on social networks of great diversity.

After the Mexican-American War, William Heath Davis, a hide and tallow merchant, and rancher Miguel Pedrorena developed a "new town" San Diego several miles south of the pueblo on San Diego Bay, believing the town would be a terminus for Southern cotton shipping. It failed with the Lost Cause. In 1867, Alonzo Horton, a wealthy San Francisco furniture merchant, bought Davis' failed town site and the coastal plain south of Old Town, known as Horton's Addition. He built a pier and warehouses that lined Fifth Avenue south to the bay and a luxury hotel at Third Avenue and D Street (renamed Broadway in 1910). Again, San Diegans were promised a direct railroad link from the East, but the spasmodic economy of the post-bellum period halted these plans, it seemed, indefinitely. The boom of the 1880s rekindled hope for a railroad and civic greatness, but the land boom turned to bust with spurious fortunes lost. Nonetheless, New Town resembled the frontier outpost of westward expansion. It was a get-rich-quick environment. Chinese fishermen had left railroad work and the mines of the Sierra to dominate the local fishing industry and settled in an area known as "Stingaree Town," the city vice district.

On the southwest corner of Fifth Avenue and K Street stood the First and Last Chance Saloon, the starting point of the Stingaree district, which extended westward to First Avenue and northward from K Street to Market. This lively area was filled with middle class fortune seekers and courthouse politicians, but also hucksters and confidence men, painted ladies, retired gunfighters, scallywags and wharf ruffians, saloon kings and queens, and an ever-ready vigilante squad of rural whites available to San Diego's leading citizens. They caroused saloons and gambling parlors like the Railroad Coffeehouse and Wyatt Earp's three gaming joints. The population dropped from a high of 40,000 to 16,000 people by 1890. Portuguese fishermen had arrived in Loma Portal and southern blacks found their way to the Stingaree's outer reaches at Imperial Avenue in search of freedom. At the turn of the twentieth century, San Diego maintained first-rate establishments, commercial districts, and buildings grouped around the area of Fifth and G Street, but working class neighborhoods ringed the downtown with an economy of labor power, entertainment, and vice.

The first two decades of the twentieth century saw significant growth in San Diego County, with the downtown moving northward to the intersection of Fifth and Broadway. San Diego held 39,578 people by 1910. The central business district became somewhat respectable with George Marston's department store, real estate offices (particularly that of Ed Fletcher), and the completion of the luxurious U.S. Grant Hotel in 1910 on Horton Plaza. The Civic Improvement Committee, led by George Marston, hired urban planner John Nolen in 1907 to redesign commercial San Diego into an exemplar of Spanish colonial beauty. With Progressivism flourishing locally, city leaders announced in 1909 their intent to hold the Panama Exposition within Balboa Park. However, the Stingaree district had grown considerably. With business growth and anticipation of the World's Fair, the district attracted ever more numbers of the merchant marine, prostitutes, bunco men, hopheads, and the city's demimonde to its vibrant establishments. The Stingaree sported parlors, opium dens, and saloons such as the Old Tub of Blood, Seven Buckets of Blood, the Green Light, the Bullpen, Yankee Doodle Hall, Pacific Squadron Hall, the Legal Tender Saloon, the Turf, and the high-class parlor house run by Mamie Goldstein. The wharf area at Fifth Avenue was a hangout for San Diego's guano pirates, a rough lot who worked Baja's islands on fertilizer ships often owned by esteemed San Diegans.

The Stingaree contained a majority of the radical movement in San Diego (Wobblies, anarchists, socialists, and Marxists) that led the infamous Free Speech Fight from 1909-1914. The notorious soapbox orations of the local radical movement were located at Fifth and E at Heller's Corner. The Mexican Revolution spread to the border in January of 1911, when Ricardo Flores Magón and the *Partido Liberal Mexicano* (PLM) captured the border town of Mexicali, then took Tijuana. This alarming event created local anxiety until 1917, and led the San Diego City Council to ban street speaking in 49 square-blocks of downtown to silence radicalism. A local vigilante committee composed of leading citizens and their henchmen formed to battle labor militants in the Stingaree. They intimidated local social progressives and labor leaders with terrorist threats and physical harm.

The situation appeared threatening enough from 1914 to 1916 that William Tompkins, secretary of the Chamber of Commerce, asked Governor Hiram Johnson to mobilize the state militia, explaining that "here we are convinced that the situation is grave enough and respectfully urge that you take immediate and favorable action for our protection." Edward Stahle, the new chamber secretary, pleaded with Johnson to protect lives and property in 1916 because of "the imperative necessity of guarding the Mexican border line from ocean to Imperial Valley—Mexicans becoming restless [and] are congregating and growing arrogant." With an unlikely revolution at hand, the city council empowered Walter Bellon, the city health inspector, to raze the heart of the Stingaree through building and health surveys. To redeem the image of San Diego before millions of tourists traveled to the exposition, the City Health Department demolished 120 buildings and condemned 500 rooms in the Stingaree. Many lucrative and tax-generating businesses, though morally suspect, were forever destroyed. It did not stop working-class entertainments, prostitution, or vice, but merely moved it all "uptown," or closer to the business district at Fifth and Broadway. Through fervent reform, San Diego Progressives laid the historical foundations for the city's diverse social networks located along Broadway down south to the Gaslamp Quarter.

During the 1920s, San Diego grew significantly as a younger bumper crop of entrepreneurs and Midwestern retirees sought to live the Golden State lifestyle of health and repose. San Diego led the way in 1919 when the All-Year-Club of San Diego, founded by Oscar Cotton, sang the city's song. And Broadway became the premier boulevard of the nouveau riche. The new men of wealth, however, ceded the city to the Navy Department, remaking downtown San Diego into "sailor town." But the money generated from the naval infrastructure brought John Nolen back to San Diego in 1925 to plan for downtown and general civic beautification. Writing from Nice, France, in October of 1926, Nolen told Marston how southern France reminded him "again and again of Southern California, especially San Diego. That region is full of suggestion for the development of the waterfront, parks, boulevards, play space, public buildings." From 1925 to 1937, Mayor John L. Bacon, the city council, and the park commission re-instituted piecemeal the 1908 Nolen Plan like the waterfront civic center, preservation of Presidio Hills Park, and a general plan to modernize Balboa Park. With Prohibition keeping sailor town at bay until 1933, downtown remained in the hands of the nouveau riche, with speakeasies, vaudeville theaters, and dance halls barely besmirching the area. But the inter-war years brought significant numbers of Italian and Mexican-Americans to San Diego to work in the local canning and fishing industries, and downtown catered to their daily needs.

Visiting chroniclers, however, painted San Diego as the backwater of the United States, where civilization dropped off the continent. Edmund Wilson, the besotted tastemaker of modern letters, brought his acerbic pen to bear on San Diego in 1932. West

Coast cities lacked the emotions and moods necessary for great American cities. For Wilson, San Diego became "The Jumping-Off Place," the literal dead-end of the American Dream. Walking the streets of downtown San Diego, he believed the city suffered from a cheap re-creation of high culture with its little business blocks, one-star hotels, and real estate offices. Wilson lamented the city had no cultural core, only enervated, status-conscious club women among dying retirees and pulmonary disease patients. With great glee, Wilson dubbed San Diego the "suicide capital" of the United States, where the little men and women "stuff up the cracks of their doors and quietly turn on the gas-drive their cars into dark alleys, get in the back seat and shoot themselves," among other ghastly deeds. Under their sunny dispositions, San Diegans were a morose lot. "Here our people, so long told to 'go West' to escape from ill health and poverty, maladjustment and industrial oppression," Wilson noted with sarcasm, "are discovering that, having gone West, their problems and diseases remain and that the ocean bars further flight." Vividly painting the San Diego cultural landscape as pathological, Wilson believed San Diegans had "come to the end of their resources in the empty California sun."

It was remarkable that a provisional bourgeois radical like Wilson missed the labor turmoil racking San Diego, especially from the local Communist Party, Trade Union Unity League, Unemployment Council, and Cannery Worker's Union (UCA-PAWA). After Prohibition, downtown transformed into a hardcore sailor town. The *WPA City Guide* for San Diego noted that south of Broadway was "one of the play areas of the navy enlisted man," a Trocadero of "hash houses and honkytonks, drinking parlors with jazz bands and tiny dance floors, trinket shops, shooting galleries, and the ever present pawnshop." These working class businesses revived the Stingaree district of the 1910s "to make 'south of Broadway' a distinct area." With the coming of World War II, the honky-tonk of downtown San Diego defined a city turned upside down by Southern Plains migration.

Wartime San Diego grew from 203,341 to 362,658 people from 1940 to 1944. The population explosion of war production created a pressure-cooker social environment in the city. Jim Thompson's *Now and On Earth*, a wartime novel of socialist realism, captures the bleak landscape of downtown San Diego under racial violence, anti-communism, wartime housing shortages, and social dislocation. *Now and On Earth* is a story about a failed "hack writer" and aircraft industry clerk caught in a web of graft whose radical past puts him in double jeopardy. In the summer of 1940, Thompson and his family traveled from Pampa, Texas to San Diego in the Oklahoma Communist Party automobile, a gigantic four-door Plymouth donated by Woody Guthrie. Recently fired as director of the Oklahoma Federal Writer's Project for his communist politics, he took a job at Ryan Aeronautical scraping paint off the floor, and he ultimately became an inventory clerk. He later worked as a timekeeper for Solar Aircraft. The Thompsons lived in a small Spanish mission duplex in Middletown at 2130 Second Avenue, a hilly neighborhood wedged between downtown San Diego and Balboa Park. It also had commanding views of San Diego Bay and the Pacific Ocean. Despite the natural beauty of the city, San Diego's diversity and cultural fusion fascinated Thompson under the stress of wartime competition and scarcity.

Often prone to periodic drinking binges in the San Diego Rialto, Thompson described the alienation and the broken dreams of war workers found in places like Eddie's Bar, the Bomber Café at 849 Broadway, and other downtown jazz clubs, dance halls, and juke joints. With the city filled with sailors at all hours, downtown was a 24/7 environment of cafes, restaurants, and entertainments. Many of the dance halls were fronts for prostitutes and drug dealers, who made their living from the meager wages of young servicemen. For Thompson, the difference between work in the war industry and the leisure found downtown had eroded, offering only new forms of degradation and exploitation. Portuguese and ethnic Mexicans stand as the only redeemable characters in the novel, generous and non-materialistic to a fault. In the end, *Now and On Earth* opposed the orthodoxies of Marxism to argue that ordinary people deserved social democracy in their own lifetime due to the human indignities caused by a country at war.

Downtown San Diego flourished as an economy for the marginal from 1945 to the 1980s, filled with locker clubs, burlesque theaters, beer bars, cocktail lounges, tattoo parlors, old men's rooming houses, and pornography shops. The business district at Fifth and Broadway still existed, but shared downtown with the poor, addicted, and unemployed. After World War II, downtown's underemployed Pacific veterans were often some of the first cases of methamphetamine addiction in the United States. Enlisted men could change from uniforms to street clothes in West Broadway locker clubs such as The Seven Seas, the Four-O, Salty's, and the Harbor. With an array of entertainments, the locker clubs also took mail for sailors, cashed checks, and offered some social grounding when men came into port. With unlimited suburban land development, some of San Diego's important businesses moved uptown. West Broadway went into economic decline when the Navy stopped docking ships at the Broadway pier in 1969. The area attracted low-income amusements, like the Green Goddess, Show Place Nudity Dance Hall, and a plethora of massage parlors for the enlisted man.

Working class and marginal institutions symbolized the economic decline of downtown by the 1970s as Vietnam War demobilization shocked the local economy. For mentally ill or displaced veterans, the Rialto economy and SRO hotels offered a sense of community during an era of political skepticism and high unemployment. Neil Morgan, San Diego's epic chronicler of social life, called the area "Back of Broadway." With sensitive eyes, he believed that this Rialto economy, though neither upscale nor respectable to some, had a rich history that connected San Diego's past and present. He described SRO hotels like the Golden West, the Aztec Theater, downtown's most popular burlesque club known as Bob Johnston's Palace Buffet, and the cafeterias and other institutions that downtowners called home. Like the days of the Stingaree, these were important cash and tax-generating businesses for the city during times of municipal budget cuts. When downtown redevelopment began in 1981, the city condemned Bob Johnston's The Sports Palace and the Hollywood Burlesque House at 1111 East Broadway. They had anchored the boulevard since 1944. Their departure enabled the redevelopers to clean up Broadway for Horton Plaza, a retail mall with parking garages facing the fabric of the city.

Whenever I walk up and down Broadway today, from the ferry landing to Interstate 5, I note that much has changed from the sailor town of my childhood. During the 1980s and 1990s, high-rise construction reoriented Broadway towards business use once again. At the corner of Broadway and Kettner Street sits the enormous Helmut Jahn building with a downtown trolley hub, right across the street from the Amtrak Station. Back in my high school days, the spot was popular for skateboarding because of the slick, marble sidewalk in front of the beer and go-go bars there. It was also a part of West Broadway that maintained social networks of great diversity; you could sit there on a weekend night and see the spectrum of humanity come and go throughout the evening, rich, poor, and in-between. One of the first times I ever learned about the Vietnam War, from a veteran no less, was on that corner. The neighborhood around West Broadway was a literal campground for homeless veterans during the 1980s, after the Jarvis/Reagan revolution cut veterans benefits and sent many onto America's streets.

Now you see commuters coming and going, wealthy professionals from downtown condominiums walking their dogs, fauxhemians crawling through the nighttime. Although downtown redevelopment has been a financial success, the old has been thrown out with the new. There are very few establishments left downtown for a younger person like myself to connect the city's past and present. Some come to mind, like the Chinese Historical Society at Third and J and many historical structures on the National Historic Register like the Horton Grand Hotel. But downtown's history is buried under the current consumer spectacle, barely noticeable. With little of historical interest to view anymore, I'll head into Wahrenbrock's Books at Eighth and Broadway, get something to read, and head down to the Hong Kong, an old beer bar. Mona, the Korean manager of the bar, will greet me with "nice to see you again." An old timer will strike-up a conversation with the words, "Let me tell you what is was like in the old days." With few of these downtown denizens to tell *their* story, I will put my book down and open my ears to this living history.

The Hong Kong Nightclub

Photo by Eugene W Brown

Ioanna Warwick
San Diego in Late October

A leaf lay at the corner of F and Eighth,
where drunks sway, sometimes relieve themselves against the
old beige walls of the Public Library.
A neatly dressed, middle-aged woman, pear-shaped, still juicy
with estrogen, and no stranger to beauty parlors,
gestured toward the leaf:
So, are you coming back at six o'clock?

The leaf was silent.
She insisted, a grudge gravelling her voice:
Are you coming back?
The leaf didn't even shrug.
She walked away into her leafless life.

I know the heartless impulse we all have,
to say to that woman, "Lady,
this leaf is never coming back. Never, never, never."
But why hasten her disappointment?
Charity requires that we wish
the leaf to ring her doorbell at six,
not tarnished and trampled-on, but perfect, Plato's leaf,
having been to Plato's beauty parlor,
dressed in metaphysical gold, crimson igniting its veins.

May it kiss her on the neck, or wherever
she likes to be kissed, and men cannot remember,
though you tell them and tell them and tell them,
thirty years of marriage—
Let her be in luck at last, the dreamed-of
lover at her door in the autumn of her years.

Sarcastic reader, this is what you think:
by evening the leaf will be gone, its dishonored
flesh flattened to a stain. As women do,
she'll be waiting for that leaf to come back
long past six; past sixty, past seventy,
in perpetual Penelope season—
past eighty even, rose highlights in her hair,
double strand of pink pearls, still waiting.

No one talks to fallen leaves in my neighborhood,

near the Church of God of Chula Vista.
The God of Chula Vista is a god of lawn mowers.
Leaves are bagged and dispatched to their fate.
Our weather is made of light: sunshine, sunshine, sunshine.

David Reid
Where I Came in

> Almost everyone still lived—it seemed to them—
> as they always had, surrounded by a material
> culture that appeared likely to last for genera-
> tions, though in fact surprisingly little of it has
> survived.
> —William L. O'Neill, *American High: The Years of
> Confidence, 1945-1960*

The landscape of one's early childhood seems eternal, yet even to a child's eye there was something provisional about the arrangements in East County, San Diego, around the mid-point of the last century—the elements were so heterogeneous.

Spring Valley, where my family moved in September 1949, along with neighboring Casa de Or, was a half-pastoral jumble of orange, avocado, and lemon groves, roadhouses, Quonset huts, the somber churches of the mainstream Protestant faiths and Pentecostal storefronts, a turkey farm, a creek that swam, or rather crawled, with crayfish. It was the month when Harry Truman informed the nation, by mimeograph distributed to the press, that the Soviets had an atomic bomb. (The People's Republic of China was proclaimed on October 1.)

Smudge pots were dramatically lit in the groves during winter frosts, and in the spring, it was an event to watch the sheep being shorn in a lot across from the gray stone Quaker church down the street. In season, we bought lugs of tomatoes, still warm from the vines, from what we called the "Japanese Gardens," tended by Issei and Nisei families not that long since returned from the internment camps. (My first best friend was a boy named Tommy Takahashi, whose parents' greenhouses were close by. But few Japanese returned to the land after the war, and the Takahashis soon enough sold theirs and moved away.)

Bungalows built by retirees from the Midwest in some imme-morial past sat on big lots, shaded by olive and pepper trees. The not-infrequent sight of one of these immemorial dwellings being unceremoniously jacked off the ground to be mounted on a huge truck and transported across the valley never failed to excite and alarm me. Nothing was forever in the golden land—not even the land, which was—and it sometimes seems, is ever more—subject to abrupt alteration by earthquake, flood, fire, and pertinacious developers. It was only the procession of the seasons, foolishly characterized as being without nuance or even as nonexistent by outlanders, which sustained the aspect of eternity. Carey

McWilliams in his classic *Southern California Country* (1946): "Actually, Southern California has two springs, two summers, and a season of rain. The first spring—the premature spring—follows closely upon the early rains in the late fall. In November the days shorten, the nights become cooler, the atmosphere clears (except when the brush fires are burning in the hills), the air is stilled, and the land is silent. By November, people have begun to listen for rain." As inexact memory goes, this is where I came in, one of the false springs of the mid-century, in the time of the polio scares.

In San Diego County, the larger movement of population after the war was inland. Reflecting their rural southern and heartland roots, most of the war workers, as they were frankly called in those days, who had come to San Diego to work in the aircraft assembly plants during the war, turned their backs on the sea. My father had grown up on a farm in the Texas hill country, my mother in a Greek community in Salt Lake City. The beaches were for the rich, the young and the raffish; I suspect that many people of my parents' age and background considered the seashore faintly unhealthy as well as being definitely seedy in the affordable range. (Mildew featured prominently in their discussions when my parents considered but rejected a house in Point Loma.) My mother regretted the move from our little house on G Street, near downtown, missing the metropolitan principle. Streetcars still ran down Broadway to the harbor, across town to North Park and Hillcrest, and daily life maintained some of the bustling tempo of wartime. Now we were moving—not to the suburbs, which came later, with the freeways and ranch houses—to the sticks.

Spring Valley had belonged to no historic rancho, and had nothing to do with the well-advertised (in those days) Mission Romance, so beloved of newspapers with Anglo proprietors like the *San Diego Union* and the *Los Angeles Times*. Curiously, the one site of any antiquarian interest was the house where the historian Hubert Howe Bancroft, who ran a Dickensian word factory in San Francisco in the nineteenth century, had once lived; a friend's parents were the caretakers, and I often walked there through the enticing jungle of bamboo trees. Apart from the Bancroft House, Spring Valley boasted no landmark comparable to Lemon Grove's famous concrete lemon ("Best Climate on Earth") and lacked either the urban density of El Cajon, which had a proper downtown with a department store and movie theater, or the gentility of La Mesa, which is favorably noticed in the WPA's *California: A Guide to the Golden State* (1939), which declares: "La Mesa is a city of homes. In the surrounding foothills are fine estates. . . . La Mesa has an annual fall flower festival. At La Mesa the highway enters the level coastal plain."

I can imagine the interiors of the houses on those fine estates. Such architectural grandeur as one encountered in those days was in the funereal style (brass fittings, red curtains, high slitted "Moorish" windows) that furnish the décor of novels by James M.Cain and *The Day of the Locust*. The style my parents called "modernistic" did not flourish in the East County.

The most imposing house in our vicinity was a half-timbered Tudor commanding a hilltop above Lemon Grove that had been brought over from England in the Twenties, rumor said by a prosperous bootlegger. Here my future wife Darcy Cremer, her brother and four sisters were raised, and we were married. There were stables and a swimming pool on the grounds. "No horses!" were the only words of advice my polyphiloprogenitive father-in-law, who had worked on the Manhattan Project at Los Alamos during the war, ever gave me about child-rearing, and now to my wonder and dismay, epochs later, the house is a museum, an artifact maintained by the municipality, like the lemon.

Half a hundred years ago, we lived in a compact province of Southern California Country, bounded on the south by the Mexican border, which we rarely crossed, on the west by the beaches—the choppy waves at Pacific Beach, placid Coronado Beach with its Ozymandian hotel (thus, Frank Baum's Oz?), and by Harbor Drive, along which stretched the mile-factory, Convair's Plant 1, where bombers and airliners were assembled, and my father worked. It was famous that during the war the plant had been ingeniously disguised at roof level as a village complete with steepled church, thus to deceive Japanese bomber pilots. But equally imposing was corporate headquarters, a huge square monolith of a building, known locally as "The Rock," which had been built without windows for the safety of the bureaucrats within, in case the Japanese were not deceived. The overwhelming fact of the Second World War loomed like a Chinese wall in those days. Now we were launched on an interminable Cold War for which corporate headquarters seemed an equally fitting command post. In *All That Is Solid Melts Into Air*, Marshall Berman writes that when he and his friends in New York discovered the frightful visage of Moloch in Allen Ginsberg's *Howl*:

> Moloch whose eyes are a thousand blind windows! Moloch whose skyscrapers stand in the long streets like endless Jehovahs! Moloch whose factories dream and croak in the fog! Mololch

whose smokestacks and antennae crown cities!

—they "thought once" of New York's daemonic "Master Builder," Robert Moses, the destroyer of the Bronx. But discovering Howl in the basement of Wahrenbrock's Books on Broadway, a few years later, I thought at once of the monolith on Harbor Drive.

To the north was the babylonish immensity of Los Angeles. The way there was through the opulent village of La Jolla and the endless aromatic orange groves off Orange County. Jack Kerouac in a journal entry, summer 1950: "San Diego rich, dull, full of old men, traffic, the sea-smell—Up the bus goes thru gorgeous seaside wealthy homes of all colors of the rainbow on the blue sea – cream clouds – red flower – dry sweet atmosphere – very rich, new cars, 50 miles of it incredibly, an American Monte Carlo." Unsung Jacumba had made a vivider impression: "birds at misty & a man walking out of the trees of Mexico into the American sleepy border street of shacks & trees & backyard dumps) – (Future place for me)," he adds. La Jolla was a whited sepulcher, the country of old men; Mexico the country of history's inheritors, the eternal peasant fellahin.

Almost all the relevant part of Southern California Country could be seen, Pisgah-like, from our local peak of Mount Helix, whose 1,380 feet were surmounted by a thirty-foot-high cross. "The name was suggested by the corkscrew road that winds to the summit," informs the *WPA Guide*, "where there is a view of San Diego and the Pacific Ocean." On a clear day the rolling green hills and coastal plain stretched limitlessly toward the Pacific, defined sometimes by a glow on the horizon, a sight as vast as a planet.

Literally, as I now understand, this was a visionary landscape, whose architecture, horticulture, and landscaping, as Kevin Starr tells in his masterful *Americans and the California* series, had recreated a desert place according to the "cultural metaphors" that generations of poets and promoters, literary travelers and ambitious developers had, more or less persuasively, laid upon it: thus, California as the new Greece and California as Henry James's "primitive plate of Italy"; California as Palestine and as Paradise Regained (and perennially lost). All nostalgias, therefore all sad. Christopher Isherwood, in 1947: "California is a tragic land, like Palestine, like all Promised Lands."

To the extent I was aware of them, I found all of these tropes plausible because the movies, in which Southern California stood in for all the landscapes of the world, confirmed them. Alan Dwan, or some other silent-era auteur with a megaphone, had directed one-reeler Westerns in Lemon movies on afternoon matinees on television, I found it perfectly natural that Little Caesar and his cronies would flee down Chicago avenues lined with palm trees, although I have since learned that critics who grew up in places like Detroit—or Chicago—detected an anomaly.

According to family lore, I urgently wanted to move to the house in Spring Valley after scouting it with my father and seeing a television set, which at the age of three I assumed would come with the property. As it turned out, 1949 was exactly when the lights began to go out in the Gutenberg Galaxy. A million sets were manufactured that year, as compared to the 6000 that were operating in the entire country in 1945, a very large number of those in bars in New York City. There was, however, a pause during the Korean War when the FCC ceased to allow new frequencies, with the effect that network television remained a phenomenon confined to big cities, mostly in the northeast and the West Coast. In San Diego, even after my parents finally succumbed to the *Zeitgeist* and bought a set around 1953, a great deal of the programming seemed to consist of test patterns. In the meantime, we continued to pay attendance, though less faithfully as time went on, to the old movie temples downtown, the Orpheum and the wonderfully baroque Fox, also to the boxy neighborhood houses, and sometimes the surreal-seeming drive-ins, which were just coming in, their screens so vast they portioned out the night.

In 1952 a housing tract, Brookside, sprang up just to the west, the first salient of suburbia into the valley. I imagine, or think I remember, my father driving us over in our Studebaker on one of those days—pennants whipping in the wind, glad-handing salesman greeting eager couples, small children in tow, at the door of a tastefully appointed "model home," that form one of the standard tableaux of the Eisenhower age. The houses in Brookside were small, boxy, pastel-colored, built to three or four barely distinguishable configurations, and, once sold, immediately supported a forest of television antennae. (The development prospered, and I am told that the houses, perhaps with some illicit enlargement, now sell for upwards of $455,000.) Just after the war, poets, philosophers, and sage social scientists had pondered what the "pattern" would be of the postwar new age—the word was ubiquitous, like the more learned "paradigm" a few years later (Thomas Kuhn's gift to discourse). Now with a general in the White House for the first time since the Civil War era ("and the Republic summons Ike,/the mausoleum in her heart," Robert Lowell sang on "Inauguration Day, January 1953), with an antenna on every roof, with the schools swarming with the entirely unexpected (to demographers) numbers of the "baby boom," it was becoming possible to discern the shape of things to come, as disclosed by the gray light that shone at night from every little house.

With its sinuous streets sweeping around the postage-stamp lots, Brookside was like a miniature of the vast suburban mazes in Los Angeles, the "Ultimate City," of which the Spanish philosopher Julian Marias wrote at this time: "The huge city is thus fragmented into millions of units, solitary and uncommunicative entities. Los Angeles is a city that ought to have been founded by Leibnitz: the lights, those uncounted stars in the metropolitan sky that a plane reveals, are windowless monads, united, coordinated, and linked by that form of preordained harmony called television."

To my indignation, we did not move to Brookside or to any other standardized suburb, and remained in what I now considered our objectionably old house. Soon abandoned, I am happy to say, my childish prejudice was in accord with the times and, in most places, with these. According to Daniel Solomon in his excellent *Global City Blues*, along with breeding prodigiously, humankind since 1945 has added as much to the built environment as all the preceding seventy-something generations since it began at Sumer. Thus, that part of the material culture of the Forties that has survived the neglect, real-estate speculation, and generally misguided utopian impulses of the last sixty-odd years—the old masonry buildings, stores with false fronts, that combination of brick and neon that had a mysterious emblematic significance for Jack Kerouac—now stands literally in the shadows. After an interval of a few years between visits to San Diego, in 2003, I found downtown dominated by hotel towers in the style of Miami Beach—or was it Chicago? On Harbor Drive, only a sad remnant of the old assembly plants that won the war were left, and it was obvious that the combination of tropical foliage, even banana trees, and Bauhaus-severe architecture that had once seemed so futuristic would not last much longer. Even "The Rock" seemed less imposing, subdued to the peaceful purposes of the harbor authority, if memory serves. My old East County neighborhood was now crowded with dingbats, and of course the groves were mostly memories. And slowly, the metaphorical strata of the older material culture—the Southern California that was meant to recall, or to impersonate, Greece, or Italy, or Palestine—is buried beneath an architecture that aspires to a placeless contemporaneity, becoming less accessible than the ancient models themselves.

In the first year of this century, my wife, Jayne, and I were traveling in Greece with our friend Nikolas Koskoros. Driving across the Peloponnesus on our way to Messenia (Nestor's Palace), we stopped in Argos, which has sat on the Argolid plain

for over five thousand years, and is supposed to be the oldest con-
tinuously occupied site in Greece. (The head of Medusa is buried
somewhere near the marketplace.) In its present incarnation a
business-like trading center with a fine nineteenth-century
church and splendid square, the Plateia Agios Petro, Argos is
where my mother's family lived—forever, they say, because like
Athenians, Argives are autochthons, whose ancestors claimed to
spring from the soil—until just before the First World War, when
my grandparents and their friend, who married my grandmother
after my grandfather died, left for America.

Toward dusk we climbed up to the ancient citadel, known
since medieval times as the Castle of Larissa—a haunting sprawl
of Byzantine, Frankish, Venetian, and Turkish fortifications built
on Mycenean foundations that were a thousand years old when
Pausanias, that indefatigable travel writer, visited in the second
century A. D. "A poem! a poem!" Nikolas said, as we reached the
summit. I would like to think I had the wit to recite the famous
chorus from Shelley's "Hellas" that for some reason I memorized
as a boy, perhaps to be prepared for such an occasion:

> The world's great age begin anew,
> The golden years return,
> The earth doth like a snake renew
> Her winter weeds outworn;
> Heaven smiles, and faiths and empires gleam
> Like wrecks of a dissolving dream.

Far below, in the gathering dark, the green plain of Argos
stretched toward the Argolikos Gulf and the sea.

Mel Freilicher

One or Two Things I Know About Kathy Acker

On the eve of her death in a Tijuana cancer clinic, her publisher Ira Silverberg, editor-in-chief at Grove Press, called again, this time trying to locate Kathy's illegitimate twins: he had been told about them by Kathy's cousin, Pooh Kaye, the dancer. Elly Antin answered the phone. After initial incredulity, she kind of thought she remembered hearing something about one of them. (Much of Elly's rich artistic life has entailed creating dazzling and durable superstructures for her own deepest fantasy personae.) *One twin*? I had known Kathy since we were college freshmen together, and I could assure them both that no such offspring existed. Several days later, Kathy's second husband, Peter Gordon, the composer, e-mailed a mutual friend inquiring into the whereabouts of said twins, having also talked to Pooh Kaye. Kathy and Peter had lived together for seven years in the '70s, on both coasts (they married a month before splitting up): the twins allegedly originated prior to their meeting.

I find it remarkable that these individuals, who knew Kathy intimately at various points in the '70s, and some afterwards, should grant even momentary credibility to this tale of the twins. The willingness to suspend disbelief, on the part of people who undoubtedly have a healthy dose of skepticism regarding virtually all other matters, can be seen as a tribute to the urgency of what Kathy represented to all of us. That is, expansive and transformative possibilities, and the primacy of imagination, or the malleability of reality in its mighty wake. (Twins have a definite resonance, being connected to Dionysius and the dual nature of the Roman god Mercurius, a key figure for alchemists. Pindar wrote about twins living one day in the underworld and one in the world above.)

I don't intend to analyze these individuals here, but their reactions seem to speak to complex emotional states at Kathy's death, including an uncharacteristic gullibility, and desire to perpetuate her legendary status as well as a living connection with her. I myself managed to refrain from embellishing the rumor, though I toyed with the idea of claiming paternity for the late Herbert Marcuse, eminent Marxist philosopher: the original rumor came replete with nameless professor lover/twin progenitor. Kathy had first moved to San Diego in 1966, after her sophomore year, when she married Bob Acker (an epic in itself, in which Acker was at the apex of a torrid triangle); Acker, more a self-styled nihilist than leftist, followed Marcuse from Brandeis to grad school at UCSD.

In some senses, the rumor could appear credible: Kathy was widely experienced, extremely sophisticated, very mobile, and later highly influential in numerous international arts and community circles. And utterly uncompromising. Kathy's life and work were a piece in the absolute rigor with which they opposed smothering and authoritarian conventions and platitudinous, bourgeois morality. As the press release for her L.A. memorial at Beyond Baroque so correctly stated:

> A ferocious, brilliant, and groundbreaking artist reflecting and assaulting post-innocence America...Acker was a visionary in the traditions of Rimbaud and Burroughs, dedicated to the possibilities of a revolutionary writing that rages against every authority, fiction, and creed, then keeps on going.

Kathy's writings are deeply involved with *embracing others' experiences*, while rendering and recontextualizing her own within "appropriated" worlds of cultural carnage, and also of a gloriously sustaining literary heritage. (She disliked the term "appropriation": "I just do what gives me most pleasure: write. As the Gnostics put it, when two people fuck, the whole world fucks.") Kathy's carefully constructed public image often seemed wrong: deceptively egocentric, way too one-dimensional. That was largely due to forces outside her control, such as the otherwise excellent publication *RE/SEARCH's* ridiculous *Angry Women* issue. (As if 95% of the world's population isn't in a rage, or wouldn't be if they weren't too exhausted and heavily narcoticized.)

Those who were only familiar with the neo-punk or neo-primitive images—who usually hadn't read any of her books—tended to be astonished at Kathy's delicate and well-bred drawing room manners, and formidable conversational skills. These coexisted with many salient qualities, including wildness (à la *Wuthering Heights*); solipsism; a lifetime of thrilling, avaricious reading and passionate intellectual pursuits; obsessive and masochistic tendencies, which unfortunately could not always be confined to the sexual realm, where they afforded her vast pleasure.

Certainly, dramatically varied life experiences were integral to Kathy's rough evolution from Sutton Place to declassé Bohemian, in which she plays a heroine straight out of the deepest novelistic traditions of *Moll Flanders, Vanity Fair*, and preeminently, the Brontës. After her marriage to Acker, Kathy basically had no con-

tact with her family—before that, they had sent her to the finest
(and Waspiest) New York private girls' schools and otherwise
ignored her—till many years later when she inherited a good deal
of money from her grandmother. This era included multiple abor-
tions, visits to "free clinics" (along with occasional futile phone
requests to her mother for money to go to a doctor), and way too
many prolonged, painful outbreaks of Pelvic Inflammatory
Disease, requiring much bed rest—one direct link to Kathy's sub-
sequent love of bodybuilding and motorcycle riding.

Speaking of the legend, her employment then was largely in
the wacky world of "adult entertainment." In San Diego, she
rather happily worked as a stripper in several downtown joints
and elsewhere (a van took them on a nightly circuit). Most of the
people we knew who were out of grad school (Kathy lasted about
five minutes in that stultifying atmosphere) had unenviably
hideous jobs like room service waiter or editing slick and bogus
textbooks for CRM, publisher of Psychology Today ad nauseum.
Kathy, aka "Target," would do an interpretative strip to "Ché," by
Ornette Coleman I believe, after carefully explaining to the audi-
ence of mostly sailors who Ché was and why he was so venerable.
(In this period she was writing under the noms de plume of RIP-
OFF RED, GIRL DETECTIVE and THE BLACK TARANTULA: when
she moved to San Francisco, most new friends called her "TBT.")
Earlier, in New York, Kathy had made some porn films and
worked for a while in a "live sex show" (i.e. simulated) in Times
Square. This gig consisted of composing then acting out skits with
her live-in lover Lenny, such as the perennially popular, dastard-
ly therapist/ingenue patient. But when Kathy was driven into a
hellish state of unbearable nightmares about leering men, she
promptly quit.

It wasn't only the slippery economic slope which suggested a
literary cast to Kathy's existence: many events were truly larger
than life. Most catastrophic was her mother's Christmas Eve sui-
cide: found dead of an overdose in a posh midtown hotel, after
disappearing for days. The suicide greatly increased Kathy's con-
siderable paranoia, and not just for obvious reasons. Prior to it,
Kathy had been hopeful about slightly better relations with her
mother. They had achieved a recent rapprochement based on the
odd circumstance of her mother suddenly becoming an habitué of
Studio 54 and even running in circles where Kathy's "under-
ground" literary reputation had some cachet. (Then, it was
assumed her mother's suicide was due to finances; now, of
course, it's impossible not to wonder about health problems.)
Kathy never learned her biological father's name. The utter dis-

tance from her stepfather seemed to reflect her mother's feelings. Kathy was once approached by a distinguished looking gentleman who claimed that she was a member of the prominent New York Lehman family. (Kathy was also related to the German-Jewish Ochs dynasty that owns the New York Times.)

Clearly, it's not easy to live out a myth, as children of the famous can testify. Many among their most unique and accomplished ranks work diligently to minimize the "destiny" quotient by keeping away from, or sharply subdividing their social and intellectual terrains from that of their parents. (Similarly, several political refugees I know with truly epic lives are resolute about normalizing daily routines, de-emphasizing and de-romanticizing their own pasts.) In her work, Kathy was brilliantly in control of that mythmaking tendency. In an essay published in 1989 in *Review of Contemporary Fiction*, she discusses the current "post-cynical" phase, in which "there's no more need to deconstruct, to take apart perceptual habits, to reveal the frauds on which our society's living. We now have to find somewhere to go, a belief..." She writes about her recently completed book, *Empire of the Senseless:*

> After having traveled through innumerable texts, written texts, texts of stories which people had told or shown me, texts found in myself, Empire ended with the hints of a possibility or beginning: the body, the actual flesh, almost wordless, romance, the beginning of a movement from no to yes, from nihilism to myth.

To me, it's an open question as to how confused Kathy herself was regarding being mythological Kathy, and how damaged by it. Her reputation as occasional diva (to the max) was well deserved. But that chiefly operated in a self-destructive manner, with friends, rather than in customary obnoxious ways: she was a revered teacher, for instance, and a courteous and personable customer. I see these issues as aligned with Kathy's contempt for therapy (and deep terror of mind control), which of course didn't prevent an exhaustive reading of Freud and Lacan—she must have been one of three or four individuals from Brandeis in the '60s who never went to a shrink! All of this speaks to the poignant questions (way beyond my scope here) of why Kathy made the apparently irrational decision to not have radiation following her mastectomy. And why, at that time, she had recourse to virtually nobody with whom to discuss these decisions rationally.

As to my personal history with Kathy, that would take volumes. We were freshmen together at Brandeis, in the (itself mythic) generation of '68. Only nodding acquaintances there, we had several close mutual friends in overlapping cliques of "hip" students (at least a third of the school). At an institution with sharp, highly eccentric, original (and image-conscious) students, Kathy Alexander stood out from the start. (Supposedly, the Ackers were represented in Michael Weller's popular play, *Moonchildren*, but we could never identify them.) One of a handful of classics majors at Brandeis, it was well-known that she entered proficient in Greek and Latin (which was astonishing to me, coming from the shitty public schools of Yonkers). Kathy seemed to live in the library, to study constantly, to devour books. Deeply intellectual, her look was vulnerable, pouty, "experienced" and sexy, somewhat androgynous.

Kathy was involved with the very coolest upperclassmen, including several in Acker's crowd who'd been in the big pot bust. The administration told them to leave for a year and seek therapy (no doubt soul-searching was also recommended). On their return, they were required to live in the dorms—that's how I came to have a rapport with Acker, who was on my floor his junior year. Kathy was quite influential with the women in our class. Working independently, she and I were chief architects of Debby Anker's gala weekend (Debby now runs the human rights clinic at Harvard Law School) of losing her virginity—with a lanky, handsome (booted and side-burned) upperclassman who drove a motorcycle and played guitar. (I had somewhat of a crush on him: I was posing as "bi" then, which was chic, though being gay was still beyond the pale.) There was the memorable occasion when Kathy half-heartedly slit her wrists. Two other women on the floor immediately followed suit. The resident advisor (who later was rumored to have joined the Weather underground) rushed into her room and insisted that Kathy stop immediately—otherwise, the whole dorm would be imitating her!

Kathy and I became close almost immediately in 1968, when I migrated from Brandeis to grad school at UCSD. Caravanning out here with friends, including her freshman roommate, Tamar Diesendruck (a painter who became a composer and won the Prix de Rome), four of us crashed on the Ackers' floor until we found a place to rent. Similar to students in Cambridge and environs, they were living in a spacious, old Victorian house with wood floors. Except to find that in So-Cal, they had to travel to an old section near downtown—and to afford it, they lived directly under the flight path at Lindbergh Field. That was over 15 miles away

from the campus, which like UC Santa Cruz, was designed dur-
ing the years of the Berkeley Free Speech Movement, for maxi-
mum distance from the city. They hitched to school (Kathy never
did learn to drive a car).

Although by no means identifying as a "hippie," Kathy baked
bread, and sewed her own clothes (a contrast to Brandeis where
she shoplifted them from Design Research): perhaps an easier
task than it appeared, since she wore the world's shortest skirts.
Acker paced constantly. They played Chess and GO; we all played
cards. (I remember a prolonged Bridge game on the floor with
Kathy, at an anti-military research sit-in.) Acker was quite
impulse-ridden. The "Passover seder" they invited us to that first
year consisted chiefly of him tying Tamar to a chair, which he sort
of danced around maniacally, till Kathy, who usually appreciated
Acker's less aggressive antics, made him desist. (I understand
that he's now a corporate lawyer.)

Primarily, then as always, Kathy was reading and writing.
Working in virtual isolation, she was the first peer I knew well to
take herself seriously as a writer. Our few models here were from
an older generation, particularly UCSD Music professor Pauline
Oliveros, and David Antin, critic and poet in Visual Arts. Kathy
fervently "apprenticed" herself (as she said) to David, auditing all
of his classes. I followed, and we became fast friends with David
and Eleanor, taking turns babysitting for their son, Blaise. Both
disgruntled with school, we had a Swift seminar together, where
we annoyed everyone by incessantly passing notes and giggling.
Highlights of our cultural life were the midnight, underground
films at a theater way out in East San Diego (which soon turned
to porn) that, amazingly, showed the likes of Brakhage and
Kuchar, and the Anomaly Factory, a water tower on campus
which a group of undergrads converted into an innovative, com-
puterized, hi-tech, theater-lab.

It was absolutely invaluable to witness Kathy's discipline and
comprehensive structuring of her time for reading and writing, as
well as self-confident experimentation and professional attitude
about getting the work out. Although UCSD was new and in many
ways vital (for a university), it was, and still is, all too easy for peo-
ple in San Diego to behave as if they're on permanent vacation:
many would-be dilettantes. Of course, what Kathy was writing
about also became crucial to me, not to mention to post-modern
thought—human identity, and how to get rid of (and/or retrieve)
it! (Maybe the twins would heroically attempt both!)

Although we were the same age, Kathy always felt that she
was a member of the younger generation of punks. (For one thing,

she was considerably less seduced by psychedelic drugs, despite occasional coke or opium binges in the old days.) We shared a deep mistrust of Utopian thinking: her chief complaint against "hippies." I was more concerned with its pernicious effects on Marxist ideology of "scientific" history and a Central Committee somehow spawning a classless society. An activist during Vietnam, afterwards I worked mostly with artists coalitions and organizations staging multi-media shows downtown (and attacking local "poverty program pimps" cum FBI agents). For 15 years, I also published CRAWL OUT YOUR WINDOW, a regional San Diego arts/literary magazine. (One pole of my Brandeis identity had been participating in many civil rights sit-ins, and anti-war marches. A member of CORE in high school, the summer after I graduated, I grew a beard in order to have my freshman image in place for the fall.)

Kathy was extremely supportive of such organizing activities. Certainly she shared the central axioms of our time concerning the pure and incorruptible evil of post-monopoly capitalism, and all governments which serve it—which is tantamount to saying that she breathed the same oxygen as the rest of us. Traveling frequently, wherever she went—Seattle, Minneapolis, East Berlin-Kathy investigated local scenes, meeting people running presses, alternative media, food coops, independent music labels, squatters rights organizations. Our ongoing dialog on "alternative" cultures lasted a lifetime.

It's impossible to detail Kathy's significance to me. During my 20's, I was pretty much bicoastal, spending part of each year in New York. She introduced me to many artists and composers there; some became boyfriends or hot sex. We both kind of avoided other writers, but were close to Jackson MacLow and Bernadette Mayer; Kathy used to take me over to Ted Berrigan's, I'd bring her to Ashbery's. She turned me on to writers way before anyone was discussing them, especially Bruno Schulz and Elias Canetti. So many stellar individual events, like our wonderful Christmas Eve dinner at (the mobbed) Second Avenue Deli. Afterwards, getting drunk at the Astor Hotel bar, where we composed telegrams to various men whom she wanted to entice and/or tell off; I'd go to the pay phone and send them. (We also wrote telegrams to the Antins and others, requesting that they adopt us and be our family; those we didn't send.)

In terms of a sibling relationship, I was able to help Kathy in some concrete ways, in her numerous moves from city to city and coast to coast, or when she ran out of money to self-publish. As with all of Kathy's close friends, many of our longest and most hilarious conversations over the years took place late at night, when she called in great pain over a boyfriend situation. She would describe what had transpired in vivid and obsessive detail. We'd laughingly envision remedial scenes, improvise dialogs and various types of merry retribution.

There's no simple way to describe, let alone deal with the palpability of absence, which appears to be our chief Millennial legacy. Basically, for me, the short of it is this: life seems inconceivable without Kathy to properly narrate it. It seems, too, that it will always feel that way.

Mike Davis

The Perfect Fire

Sunday morning in San Diego. The sun is an eerie orange orb, like the eye of a hideous jack-o-lantern. The fire on the flank of Otay Mountain, which straddles the Mexican border, generates a huge whitish-grey mushroom plume. It is a rather sublime sight, like Vesuvius in eruption. Meanwhile the black sky rains ash from incinerated national forests and dream homes.

It may be the fire of the century in Southern California. By brunch on Sunday eight separate fires were raging out of control, and the two largest had merged into a single forty-mile-long red wall. The megalopolis's emergency resources have been stretched to the breaking point and California's National Guard reinforcements are 10,000 miles away in Iraq. Panic is creeping into the on-the-spot television reports from scores of chaotic fire scenes.

Fourteen deaths have already been reported in San Bernardino and San Diego counties, and nearly 1000 homes have been destroyed. More than 100,000 suburbanites have been evacuated, triple as many as during the great Arizona fire of 2002 or the Canberra (Australia) holocaust last January. Tens of thousands of others have their cars packed with family pets and mementos. We're all waiting to flee. There is no containment, and infernal fire weather is predicted to last through Tuesday.

It is, of course, the right time of the year for the end of the world.

Just before Halloween, the pressure differential between the Colorado Plateau and Southern California begins to generate the infamous Santa Ana winds. A spark in their path becomes a blowtorch.

Exactly a decade ago, between October 26th and November 7th, firestorms fanned by Santa Anas destroyed more than a thousand homes in Pasadena, Malibu, and Laguna Beach. In the last century, nearly half the great Southern California fires have occurred in October.

This time climate, ecology, and stupid urbanization have conspired to create the ingredients for one of the most perfect firestorms in history. Experts have seen it coming for months.

First of all, there is an extraordinary supply of perfectly cured, tinder-dry fuel. The weather year, 2001-02, was the driest in the history of Southern California. Here in San Diego we had only 3 inches of rain. (The average is about 11 inches). Then last winter it rained just hard enough to sprout dense thickets of new underbrush (a.k.a. fire starter), all of which have now been desiccated for months.

Meanwhile in the local mountains, an epic drought, which may be an expression of global warming, opened the way to a bark beetle infestation which has already killed or is killing 90 percent of Southern California's pine forests. Last month, scientists grimly told members of Congress at a special hearing at Lake Arrowhead that, "it is too late to save the San Bernardino National Forest." Arrowhead and other famous mountain resorts, they predicted, would soon "look like any treeless suburb of Los Angeles."

These dead forests represent an almost apocalyptic hazard to more than 100,000 mountain and foothill residents, many of whom depend on a single, narrow road for their fire escape. Earlier this year, San Bernardino county officials, despairing of the ability to evacuate all their mountain hamlets by highway, proposed a bizarre last-ditch plan to huddle residents on boats in the middle of Arrowhead and Big Bear lakes.

Now the San Bernardinos are an inferno, along with tens of thousands of acres of chaparral-covered hillsides in neighboring counties. As always during Halloween fire seasons, there is hysteria about arson. Invisible hands may have purposely ignited several of the current firestorms. Indeed, in Santa Ana weather like this, one maniac on a motorcycle with a cigarette lighter can burn down half the world.

This is a specter against which grand inquisitors and wars against terrorism are powerless to protect us. Moreover, many fire scientists dismiss "ignition"—whether natural, accidental, or deliberate—as a relatively trivial factor in their equations. They study wildfire as an inevitable result of the accumulation of fuel mass. Given fuel, "fire happens."

The best preventive measure, of course, is to return to the native-Californian practice of regular, small-scale burning of old brush and chaparral. This is now textbook policy, but the suburbanization of the fire terrain makes it almost impossible to implement it on any adequate scale. Homeowners despise the temporary pollution of "controlled burns" and local officials fear the legal consequences of escaped fires.

As a result, huge plantations of old, highly flammable brush accumulate along the peripheries and in the interstices of new, sprawled-out suburbs. Since the devastating 1993 fires, tens of thousands of new homes have pushed their way into the furthest recesses of Southern California's coastal and inland fire-belts. Each new homeowner, moreover, expects heroic levels of protection from underfunded county and state fire agencies.

Fire, as a result, is politically ironic. Right now, as I watch

San Diego's wealthiest new suburb, Scripps Ranch, in flames, I recall the Schwarzenegger fund-raising parties hosted there a few weeks ago. This was an epicenter of the recent recall and gilded voices roared to the skies against the oppression of an out-of-control public sector. Now Arnold's wealthy supporters are screaming for fire engines, and "big government" is the only thing standing between their $3 million homes and the ash pile.

Halloween fires, of course, burn shacks as well as mansions, but Republicans tend to disproportionately concentrate themselves in the wrong altitudes and ecologies. Indeed it is striking to what extent the current fire map (Rancho Cucamonga, north Fontana, La Verne, Simi Valley, Vista, Ramona, Eucalyptus Hills, Scripps Ranch, and so on) recapitulates geographic patterns of heaviest voter support for the recall.

The fires also cruelly illuminate the new governor's essential dilemma: how to service simultaneous middle-class demands for reduced spending and more public services. The white-flight gated suburbs insist on impossible standards of fire protection, but refuse to pay either higher insurance premiums (fire insurance in California is "cross-subsidized" by all homeowners) or higher property taxes. Even a Hollywood superhero will have difficulty squaring that circle.

Kate Savage

Yes. No. Maybe.

San Diego is burning down and I am really fucking stoned. I mean Really. Goddamn. High. I didn't mean to get this way, rocking back and forth on the couch in the livingroom staring at the water spot on the ceiling that looks like a goat with an ice cream cone because that's all I can do. I only meant to smoke a little, to take the edge off this hangover, but I ended up inhaling deeply as I watched the plastic news people telling me that the whole damn town is on fire. I try to breathe normally, to slow down my heart that is freaking out along with my mind: together on a mission for me to find the nearest bridge and jump off of it.

Nothing.

Today the sky is dark brown-red and ash has come to visit us from the hills that are presently being eaten by flames. And holy shit I am so fucking high.

This is the kind of high where I am forced, kicking and screaming, to examine just exactly why my life has become so fantastically tiresome. Revelations come barreling towards me one after another, and I can't breathe. I realize I really needn't be so self-conscious. I realize that maybe endless self-improvement is just a way to avoid improving your mind or heart. I realize I need to call my mother more often. I realize one thing after another until, finally, I have to look at the Big Thing in my life that is causing considerable grief and profuse boredom. And That Thing is upstairs in our room, playing video games like it's going out of style. That Thing is my fiancé and he's boring the shit out of me.

The destruction of things fascinates me. Whole towns burned up, gone, collapsed in on themselves. Six months with someone that felt like ten years, burned up, gone. Until there's nothing left but ashes and a few pictures.

The details are mundane—we met, drank, fucked, and then decided to give engagement a whirl three months later, what the hell. Not only are the details mundane, the whole damn relationship was mundane. The poor boy forgot how to have fun, bless his tedious heart. He couldn't understand just exactly why I didn't find extreme joy in smoking copious amounts of weed and watching old movies night after night. After night. And at first I did enjoy it, I'll admit. He was sweet and he was good to me. He cooked and never turned me down when I pressured him for sex.

But god, what a fantastic loser.

He guilted me into staying home on countless Saturday

nights. He was jealous of my friends. He told me I really should start going to the gym. He slept eighteen hours a day. He wasted untold amounts of money on bullshit—mostly overpriced DVDs of bad TV shows. I didn't know he was a computer addict when we first started dating. I thought he was mysterious, because he would disappear at weird hours of the night and stay gone for days at a time. I would jealously speculate—he's got another girl. He's got a wife. He's a CIA agent. I thought of everything but what he was really doing—playing video games at his grandmother's house.

He's twenty-seven, by the way.

I am rocking back and forth on the couch. Then I stop. Realizing what needs to be done. As soon as I understand this, I have to cry. So I do. I cry because despite all of this I really did love him. At one point I actually did consider going through with a marriage, no matter how weird it all felt. It was all so grown-up, I had a ring and everything, see? Well. Okay. Um, alright.

I walk up the stairs and into the room.

"Hey," I say.

He doesn't look up.

"We need to talk." I use a menacing tone to get his attention. He looks up and fakes innocence—all wide eyes and virtue.

"About what?" Pure as the bloody driven snow. Like he didn't know this was coming.

"About us. This isn't working. I'm not happy and god, you can't be happy. You haven't left the house in a week and a half. This has to stop." I elaborate, I am fucking clear and concise and mature about it to boot.

He laughs a weird laugh. "What are you talking about?" he says, incredulous. Like I've started speaking French all of a sudden.

Oh hell.

He does this. Every time. This is, by the way, the third time I've tried to break up with him.

"I'm talking about you. Leaving. Now."

He starts to get mad. He yells at me. He says I tricked him into loving me, and he's not leaving, and remember how I started shooting up again in the summer and I drink too much and blah blah blah. I wait until he's done. He cannot fucking touch me. I am just too stoned.

Nothing.

"Please. Get. Out." I look at him straight in the face. He looks at the ring that I haven't worn in a month with a blank face. I can feel myself starting to lose my nerve, so I leave the room and go downstairs to watch everything burn. The sorority girl neighbors are freaking out, evacuating. I vaguely entertain thoughts of looting, but then envision their apartment—what the hell could I possibly want of theirs? I imagine myself strolling out of their place with boxes of body glitter and stacks of *Vogues*, cackling at my own diabolical ways. Then I think about sleeping. I think about reading. I think about doing drugs.

Nothing, so I sit and watch the goat eat his ice cream cone. I imagine the goat has a delightfully stupid name, like Professor Goats-A-Lot or Goatrude McGoatmeister. I can hear him upstairs, moving around. Movement of the upright kind, that's a nice change of pace, there's a step in the right direction. He walks down the stairs and says he guesses he'll be going now. I feel myself start to give, to almost say forget it, let us go watch a movie, but I don't so he leaves. I sit back down.

(Nothing.)

Megan Webster

The Beast
(San Diego Wildfires 2003)

Morning breaks lead gray
glazed with bronze, ash
strewn on the ground like frost.
I choke, wheeze, close

the windows tight, fear the end
of the world. A news channel
gusts fire in my face until
my cheeks scorch. I watch flames

leap along Descanso ridge,
swallow black-beetled oaks,
eucalypti, houses, cars, power lines,
spitting cinders into Santa Ana

winds. Each day a fresh blaze—
Crest, Alpine, Paradise, Cuyamaca, Julian,
until seventeen flares torch
the county. Firefighter Rucker
fights to his end . . .

becomes my brother.
As I mop my tears, I think
of Robert Frost's *Fire and Ice*—
how I'd use the poem to teach

metaphor. Now, I see the true
face of fire, and decide
without a flicker of doubt,
that to end the world

I'd favor ice.

Art by Alessandra Moctezuma

Vote Moral Values

HOMELAND

Harold Jaffe

Things to Do During Times of War (1991)

Turn your cap back to front and root for the home team.
Don't root.
Root around in bed without a partner.
Cross dress.
Memorize military nomenclature: theater of operations, corps,
division, brigade, regiment, battalion...
Root around in bed *with* a partner, just make sure he's your
husband who's been tested and can prove it.
Flick on the TV.
Watch TV swearing at the jingoism, sentimentality and
consumer cannibalization of war.
Fling your shoe at the telegenic TV anchordroid and miss, your
shoe soaring through the empty window but being intercepted
by a Patriot anti-missile-missile in mid-flight, the impact
demolishing a crack factory in the inner city, no casualties.
Watch TV approving of the jingoism, sentimentality and
consumer cannibalization of war.
Get stoned.
Get stoned and watch the dissidents on TV throw stones and
the occupation forces shoot rubber bullets and tear gas.
Get stoned and listen to the optimistic estimates of the tens of
thousands of allied bombing *sorties* which *take out* military and
military-industrial targets but murder almost no civilians.
Carpet bombing, cluster bombing, smart bombs,
smart missiles...
Remote-switch channels to a cavalry-killing-Indians flick.
Remote-switch to pregnant women doing low-impact aerobics.
Remote-switch to a televangelist with dyed hair and two dia-
mond pinky rings closing his eyes in prayer.
Remote-switch to GI's in the desert watching videotapes of
their families.
Remote-switch to black GI's in the desert playing basketball.
Remote-switch to a fashion show featuring Gulf War Couture.
Get naked.
Look in the mirror.
Get naked and look in the mirror at the TV that is broadcasting
"news" about the war.
Stay naked, look in the mirror, stick your finger in your ass, do
a manic little dance.
Dance until you fall exhausted on the carpet.
Get a heart attack.

Get rushed to the hospital but be refused admittance for lacking
the appropriate medical coverage card.
Get rushed to another hospital but be refused admittance for
the same reason.
Get rushed to a third hospital and be admitted after the
technocrat scrutinizes your medical coverage card.
Listen to the banal conversation of the patients
who share your room.
Exchange banal conversation with the patients
sharing your room.
Exchange banal conversation while watching the war on the TV
monitor in your room.
Die in your hospital of heart failure while the TV is broadcasting
news about the war.
Don't die, get checked out of the hospital.
Return to your condo to find the bathroom window forced open
and your PC and CD stolen, but not your TV.
Return to your condo and fourteen minutes worth of phone
messages on your machine.
Swallow two Advil with sink water, sit down on the hardbacked
chair and play back the phone messages.
Flick on the TV with the sound off and return phone calls.
Ask him to come over.
Ask her to come over.
He comes over, she comes over.
They get stoned.
They get naked and look at TV news through their spread legs
in the mirror.
It's deviant but it's not fun.
They sniff each other's armpits.
They take a shower separately after not making love.
Why don't they make love?
Sex has been demoted to a tertiary urge, on a par with
dangerous, exotic travel.
Demoted by whom?
By the same TV news that presents the war.
They make cyberlove.
They drink decaf.
They part.
She removes her robe, stands in front of the mirror, and feels
her breasts for lumps.
He removes his robe, stands in front of the mirror, and feels his
testicles for lumps.
Why do they do this?
They were instructed by the same TV news that

presents the war.
He flicks on the TV in his condo.
She sits in front of the PC in her condo.
Phone rings.
It's a local veteran's group asking for money for the war effort.
It's AmVets asking for old clothes.
It's a wrong number.
It's an android breathing heavily into the phone.
It's a computer voice touting a time share in Hawaii.
It's a computer voice conducting a poll about which brand of
crazy glue you prefer.
It's not your phone, it's your fax.
It's not your phone, it's your neighbor's phone.
It's not your phone, it's the "all clear" siren on the TV.
Switch off the TV and go to sleep.
Turn and thrash, get up to pee, thrash some more,
finally fall asleep.
Die in your sleep.
Don't die in your sleep. Wake up in the morning and
flick on the TV.

Support Our Troops

Photo by Eugene W Brown

Karen K. Lewis
Nuclear Sunset Zone

Shreds of tangerine, persimmon and grape splash above the indigo sea, where dolphins arch their backs between dusk's waves. I'm in the southbound train, the *Pacific Surfliner*, heading for Solana Beach, where I will meet my father. He is recovering from his third round of chemotherapy, but I'm afraid he won't recover from the lung cancer. I am alone, because my husband is six hundred miles north, tending our children so that I might become my father's caregiver.

It's been ten years or more, since I've been on this train. The last time, my sister and I were northbound, and the train stopped unexpectedly near Oceanside, and *la migra* boarded. They rounded up a dozen suspicious people and pulled them off the train.
                                                              Shattered
Today, I notice how peacefully the pelicans glide, next to our windows, as if they don't care about the steel scars that humans have scribed across their habitat.   *dreams.*

Within this passenger car, a baby cries.   *I wish*

Children beg their tired mother for ice cream treats.
                                          that I could cry, too.
The mother takes her small children to the café car. I remember another, longer train journey with my dad. I was about five, and he rocked me in his arms, carrying me through a fever as we rode the rails from Los Angeles to South Dakota, for a family reunion. Dad gave me a stick of black licorice to settle my stomach, and he balanced me on his shoulders, strolling along the station platform when the train paused in Wyoming. My father had been smoking as I chewed on the licorice. Today, the tired mother leads her three youngsters back to their seats, where they slurp quickly melting astro-pops.

Commuters are slumped, folded into their seats like half-read newspapers. The scenery scrolls by: palm trees, stretches of sand. The moon rises now from the east, a luminous shimmer, like a pendant of abalone shell. It seems as if the moon dances in competition with the sun, while the sun becomes a sphere of mango fire, then disappears behind the Pacific horizon.

Surfers, ten, twenty, fifty surfers and swimmers lay claim to the last days of summer, which grow shorter, shorter. Waves.

Waves. Waves. An arrow of pelicans.

And the distant hum of helicopters, pulsing closer, louder,

obscuring the click-clack train song, the seagull noise, the roll of surf, the beat of my heart. Dusk patrol: three heavy-bellied marine choppers cruise at low altitude returning to Camp Pendleton.

Higher, four jet trails are illuminated like iridescent ribbons wrapping a gift of sky. What gifts are these, which my generation leaves to the next? Lovers whisper, curled into each other, across the aisle from where I sit, and their whispers, the baby crying in the back, children teasing each other in front, the executive sales manager chattering on his cell phone—all of these sounds are subordinate to the breath of the helicopters.

We pass a longer train, flat cars, slower, burdened with weight: olive-drab trucks, jeeps, brand-new armored tanks, dozens of them. Each machine is strapped down like a toy upon the shoulders of the freight cars.

A war on terror has been declared. This machinery is destined for port, where it will join other armaments and soldiers being deployed to distant lands.   *I am suddenly glad*
Why isn't it obvious that differences in belief cannot be resolved with war machines?

               that my son is barely sixteen, not old enough to join the warriors.

Steel chant of wheels on tracks: *Afghanistan, Afghanistan, Iraq, Iraq, Vietnam, Vietnam, Treblinka, Treblinka, Auschwitz.*

Palm trees fringe each sandy beach. Dolphins arch their backs between dusk's waves, swimming toward Mexico. Lights flicker on alongside the tracks, and within recreational vehicles at the campground. I wonder why so many tranquil pigeons roost on twin beige domes, built to contain radioactive contamination. Our train glides by the sign: *San Onofre.* These concrete domes resemble huge cakes, formed to celebrate the power we claim, each day, to light our lives.

The train carries me, each moment closer to reunion with my father. When I arrive, it will be dark, and I will feel safe for a moment as we hold each other, claiming the last hours of our final summer together.

DJ Watson

Clouds Over Mecca

Mecca don' be a place where Nan go. Not like Ms. Gwendolyn's Mecca on the south side of Chicago where the little boy fell down the elevator shaft in the projects and died. It's a space where she say words wail like sunshine screaming through dusty mini-blinds. She say poetry makes open wounds fill a body up and scars seal over and deliver. Nan calls it *balm* and that rhymes with calm, like me sitting on the floor cross-legged catching sunshine on the tip of my tongue. Or when I squeeze my eyes real tight, I see orange and yellow-red light floating inside me.

Nan say when she was a little girl she used to do that too, layin' on her front lawn wondering 'bout god—*was he a man, a woman, or nothing or air*-watching the sky for signs. Tracin' clouds with her fingertip—shapes like big ol' elephants and hairy buffalos and alligators and long neck giraffes. Stuff you don't normally see 'cept in cartoons. Sometimes Nan gets mad and says *why come cartoons like Lion King don't have no people only animals/what is they doing to little kids minds these days*—and I am usually coloring by then and ask Nan if she wants to color too. She say *yeah baby* and I hand her the box and we outline people and animals and sometimes we make animals that look like people and vice versa. That's how come she knows *dios es un pintor fabuloso*—that's Nan's word *fabuloso*.

Sometimes she say stuff in Spanish, 'cause she lives in San Diego, close to the border, and says we gotta learn languages so we can communicate *instead a acting like the ugly Americans we is*. I like that word *communicate*, 'cause it sound like moon and *luna* and room and sometimes me and Nan lay in her bed at night watching the moonlight draw pictures on the wall. We pretend we can fly in and out of craters in the moon's face and I trace her lips with my fingertips.

And sometime I dream I am high in the clouds and they are blue cotton candy and I take a big bite, *ummm*—no sugar, just everything good for you. I can eat as much as I want and never get full. Just me and Nan flying on the carpet in the living room, legs dangling off the side as we dip and dive—but never get dizzy, watching the world spin.

And sometime we stop, depending on if we tired or not or if we need water or if we just wanna be nosy, like curious George swinging from tree to tree at the crossroads, playin' the dozens and signifying 'til his back-bone slips and the lion catches him red-handed. Then he gotta use more than a roadmap—gotta use lies and tricks to get his self outta the middle of the cookie jar. Nan be telling stories like her daddy and his mamma before her. She say it run in the family and that's how she learned mostly everything, cause daddy Slim always say *what's the moral?* at the stories end.

We sail over Timbuktu and Djenne where scholars all over the world came to study at the great mosque, and then we fly north over Baghdad. The sky is dark and hot and it smells really bad from all the firebombs. All kinds a horrible things happenin'. Like people goin' hungry, no water or electricity and babies and little kids and grandmas and grandpas suffering. Nan clears her throat, says the *Mujahedeen turned fire worshippers to stone, topplin' they towers cause they wouldn't change they trifling ways.* I love firelight and the warm space between Nan's legs, which is the bestest place for tellin' stories. She says Baghdad's where Ali Baba and the 40 thieves lived, stealing from the treasure house, and there go Al'ed Deen, a lazy boy who got fooled by a traveling Moor who was really a *wizir.* That's a magician. And Disney done changed his name to Aladdin. Nan say *that's the first thang colonizers do*—change your birth name right before they steal your land. My name's Imani and that means faith, cause when I was born the umbilical cord was wrapped around my neck five times and I almost choked to death. But like Nan say *that's another story.*

I say *Nan, what's a colonizer?* and she says somebody like Christopher Colombus, who didn't discover 'merica or anything else. She say he got lost lookin' for spice, which was kinda like drugs back in the day. Thought he was in India, but was really in Haiti, which he named Hispaniola after Spain *cause that's who he was working for trying to get the bling-bling.* I laugh—say Nan...you ain't 'spozed to talk like that. She sucks her tongue. Say the *Taino, Caribe and Arawaks were all ready living there so how he gonna discover anythang?* And they really didn't 'preciate nobody claiming them, 'specially Queen Isabella and her boyfriend Ferdinand. And that's what colonization is—getting somebody to do your dirty work so you can stay clean like *Baby Doc and the Tonton Makout and 'merica outta be shame paying for the latest coup ousting President Aristide just cause they want to keep their strategic pearl and now they mad at Jamaica for taking him in.*

She starts coloring real hard and fast talkin' bout *Lumumba, and Malcolm and the CIA and the ghost of King Leopold roaming the Congo forest where the Mbuti people stay.* And she breaks the sunset orange and I give her rosy dawn and say—*tell me about*

Toussaint Nan—cause that calms her nerves. She say *they might have been lovers in a past life or at least good friends—it happens—* especially in Haiti where they worked black people to death on the sugarcane plantations 'cause we was cheap back then and didn't cost as much like we do now in Somalia with the Arab trade.

Slave catchers puttin' torture masks over maroon mouths so they couldn't speak or tell stories to little kids, until the people couldn't take it anymore and *Boukman led the first rebellion*. Then General Toussaint organized the people and made them drums talk and they fought 'gainst Napoleon for thirteen years—blood flowed in the streets of the Caribbean. And when the planters figured out that drums really did talk, they took them away so they couldn't *parley*, which means to chill and people had to meet on the down low to communicate. *Yeah...* I like that word.

Nan say the freedom drum was the people's heartbeat and from then on they called the island Haiti which means land of mountains in Taino-Arawak. I draw a drum and she says *uhm-hmmmmm* and starts drawing vévés on the paper, which I color in. Nan say ground signs are geometric thoughts drawn in dirt and cornmeal and she gon' be real careful and try not to break any more colors. I pat her head and say *it's okay Nan*.

She draws caravans crossing sand dunes from north Africa to India to China and Europe—Nan be having spice-road-trip-dreams like Ibn Batuta. Or like Sheherazade telling the king stories all nightlong so he won't cut off her head. For 1001 nights she ran game so tight it put him to sleep. And in the morning he was full of wine and vexed. So he spared her life 'til the following night, still wanting more 'cause one story led to the next. Nobody knows where the stories come from—but Nan say they real old. People used to sit in coffee shops and smoke the *shusha* and story tell, listenin' to bubbles from the water pipe stem, sit back, relax, sewing rubies and gems. Like Tiamat, the goddess of chaos who was wise to the end, 'til Gilgamesh got jealous and did her in. *They were some of the greatest stories ever told and it's a shame how the libraries are being destroyed and the oldest translations of the Ku' ran lost.* This time she breaks the Obsidian—*and I just keep colorin' clouds over Mecca in.*

Sue Luzzaro

Playing War
O golden child the world will kill and eat.
—Sylvia Plath

When you hold the little bullet-shaped body of a baby in your arms, swaddled in pastel colors and smelling of essence of self, skin, and soap, it's hard to see through the layers of softness straight into the hard copy DNA that says *potential for violence.* Nature vs. nurture is the paradox that teases out preferences rather than answers. I have often been stunned by the profound morality of my grandson, in particular, his ability to empathize. In his brief five years on this earth, I have seen him cry about worms and bugs that would be ground to pieces by the lawn mower, I have watched him rescue drowning bees from his wading pool, and I have known him to refuse to eat a chicken leg because he was visualizing the rest of the chicken body. And he is very clear about war play or gunplay. When I told him he shouldn't point the popgun at pets or people, he reminded me that the gun was a toy, that he was playing, and that he never, ever would really hurt anybody. When I continued on in my own vein, he asked me, "Then why did you buy this gun for me, Nonna?" His question was the beginning of this meditation.

My husband and I live on the edge of a valley that is, as yet, undeveloped. Normally, the walk down the dirt road, the birds, rabbits, sage, and wild daisies provide a little relief from the press of civilization—until recently. "Cease fire," a voice yells. Two camouflaged figures on the hill to the east of us lower their rifles. Under the heavy shag of the ancient pepper tree, we hear scurrying; then a 12-year old GI Joe parts the fringe and steps toward us. I could barely make out his facial characteristics through the mask that he wears, but he looks benign. He is apparently the leader of the rest of the paint ball platoon behind him. He reassures us that we can pass safely; his "men" will hold their fire.

The novel *Mother Night*, by Kurt Vonnegut, suggests that we should be careful about what we pretend to be because that is what we become. This idea interests me though I'm not sure to what extent I believe it. In the sixties and seventies many of us put our daughters in OshKosh overalls, or some variation on denim. The clothes were more practical, more comfortable than what many women of my generation wore as children, and there was the hope that when dressed in these clothes the girls would feel physically freer, more aggressive, that one thing would lead to another and the girls would grow up to hold their place equally beside men. But ideologically, were the overalls a flawed concept? Did we want our daughters to become Margaret Thatcher, Janet Reno? Did we want our daughters to wear three-piece suits and become dynastic CEOs? Navy pilots? And what of our sons? Perhaps we should have dressed the children uniformly in delicate dresses—exposed them all to the lessons of vulnerability.

In the time before Barbie dolls, before dolls that peed and needed diapering, my parents gave me a doll. Wearing a siren red dress, glossy brown hair and enviable curves, the doll was significant because my parents took me on an outing alone to present her to me. The doll was my gift for helping with my younger brothers and sisters on a daily basis, so my parents understood I would want nothing that was baby-like, or in any way dependent on me. I hardly ever played with that doll, though I valued it because it referred to my own value. Do the toys that we play with contribute to our identity? I believe I was shaped more by being a caregiver to my younger brothers and sisters than I was by possessing a doll. Still I wonder about the effect of donning a mock uniform, about shooting at your friends? I can't help but be suspicious of it. I also can't help but wonder if, given the money, a mother or a father in Palestine or Afghanistan or Iraq would buy toy guns and camouflage uniforms for their child.

Since the wars with Afghanistan and Iraq, more and more carloads of kids have been dropped off by busy parents to conduct paint ball wars in the canyon behind our house. The trash, the crushed soda cans, the CO2 cartridges, the paint-stained dugouts irritate me, but it's the sound of gunfire and screams throughout the afternoon, the nearness of war, that really disturbs me. My neighbors are disturbed by this too. There are practical reasons—an elderly neighbor was recently shot in the leg while walking his dog. But there are philosophical reasons as well. Most of the parents in this neighborhood are the kind who monitor the TV shows that their children watch. They are alarmed by the violence in many children's shows. By the same token, they encourage their children to watch shows like *Sesame Street* and *Barney* that promote the idea of a moral universe. The games these parents teach their children, the way they choose to discipline their children (timeouts), also suggest that they believe that children can be molded, made more pacific, and, perhaps, by extension, the larger world, as well.

In *On Human Nature*, to which I will refer several times, scientist and Nobel author, Edward O. Wilson, argues that warlike activity increases during wartime. Following the data of the anthropologist Richard G. Sipes, Wilson concludes, "the practice of war is accompanied by a greater development of combatant sports and other lesser forms of violent aggression." Nowadays, there are places you can go for "paint ball adventures." If you access www.skirmish.com, a camouflage-clad figure wearing goggles on his eyes and bushes on his head appears and points a gun at you. The web site reads: "700 acres of top-notch terrain . . . Perfect for weekend fun, corporate teambuilding, bachelor and birthday parties." The site goes on to display the various scenarios in which one could play war: the Pentagon, a fortress with towers and shooting platforms; Firebase Dewey, which is modeled after an army depot, a castle, and so on. One of the more troubling contexts for war play is called Hood in the Woods. "This is a Pocono version of a hood, with all the big trees in place. The Hood is a building to building, street fighting, game . . . It's close and intense . . . quick reflexes and sharp shooting rule." What real world event this play theater is anticipating? Again I ask, not as much for rhetorical purposes as for perspective, would a Palestinian elect to holiday at Skirmish in the Poconos?

There seems to be an inverse relationship between the desire to play war and the actual possibility of being engaged in conventional combat. War, as waged by the United States in the recent past, has come to resemble some types of play. Computer image targets, computer-programmed bombs and unmanned aerial vehicles piloted by someone on the ground wielding a yoke, stick, and rudder reflect the way technology has changed war, and mirror the way war is waged by teenagers in arcades. According to a *Defend America* news article, "Planners are using UAVs (unmanned aerial vehicles) for missions too dangerous for manned aircraft . . . UAVs can be sent to locate surface-to-air missile sites without putting crew members in harm's way." The odd paradox of technology and knowledge: At the same time that the U.S. has successfully established significant separation between weaponry and human targets, the Human Genome Project, by beginning to identify specific genes along DNA strands, reveals the fundamental similarity of one human to another. As the Project points out, "Human beings are 99.9% identical." Look through one end of technology and the human beings are closer, more intimate, a lost brother, a distant cousin—through the opposite lens and they are tiny expendable ants.

The first member of the Navy to be killed in Afghanistan was petty officer Neil Roberts. In the event of his death, Roberts had written a letter to his wife which included the following: "I died doing what made me happy...For all the times I was cold, wet, tired, sore, scared, hungry and angry, I had a blast." It's possible

that these words were written with a mind to comfort his sur-
vivors, nevertheless, they don't reflect the awesome possibility of
being killed nor the terrible probability of killing others. Rather,
his words have the surreal quality of someone participating in a
sporting event.

Further obfuscating the distinction between war and sport is
the seeming bloodlessness of the war. Both wars have been char-
acterized by an aggressive policy of de-emphasizing civilian
deaths, and it is extremely rare to see an image of civilian devas-
tation. You have to want to see these images; you have to search
them out on the Internet. We are not permitted to see even the
flag-draped caskets of American troops. *Mother Jones* carried an
article filled with pictures of American soldiers fitted with pros-
thetics, which was a rare and disturbing view of the way many
soldiers return home.

During the first World War Sigmund Freud wrote, "Thou shalt
not kill . . .. When the frenzied conflict of this war shall have been
decided, every one of the victorious warriors will joyfully return to
his home, his wife and his children, undelayed and undisturbed
by any thought of the enemy he has slain either at close quarters
or by distant weapons of destruction. It is worthy of note that
such primitive races as still inhabit the earth . . . act differently
in this respect, or did act differently until they came under the
influence of our civilization. The savage—Australian, Bushman,
Tierra del Fuegan—is by no means a remorseless murderer; when
he returns victorious from the war-path he may not set foot in his
village nor touch his wife until he has atoned for the murders
committed in a war by penances which are often prolonged and
toilsome...behind this superstition lurks a vein of ethical sensi-
tiveness which has been lost by us civilized men."

About veterans of the current wars, I cannot personally say,
but about veterans of Vietnam, Freud had it wrong. During the
Gulf War there was a campaign to honor the returning military
personnel. Yellow ribbons were tied around trees, fences, and
street signs to honor the returning heroes. The media spin at the
time was that these veterans were not going to be treated like
Vietnam veterans who were spit upon. A number of the people I
went to high school with, or am friends with now, served in
Vietnam in the early years of the war, and their return was quite
different. It was, in fact, "ethical sensitiveness" that caused these
men, when they came back from Vietnam, to grow their hair long,
and march in contingents of Vietnam Veterans Against the War.
One of the strongest memories I have of that time was sitting in a
smoke-filled apartment listening to the Chambers Brothers

singing, "The time has come today." My friend had just returned from a tour of duty as a marine in Vietnam, and we were in awe of him. Due to his experiences, due to the simple fact that he had been out of the United States, he inhabited a vastly more mature world than we did. He preferred not to talk about Vietnam, but he told us that afternoon: "We had no business shooting people, or water buffaloes; we have no business being there." This friend, among others, spent years trying to expiate the nightmares of Vietnam.

After the war on Iraq began, a craze for little green plastic soldiers swept my grandson's kindergarten. Thirty characters could be acquired for $1.59, a refreshingly cheap toy. Little boys, my grandson included, returned to lying on the ground, patiently setting up their side of the battle. Wilson asks, "Are human beings innately aggressive? This is a favorite question of college seminars and cocktail party conversations, and one that raises emotion in political ideologues of all stripes. The answer to it is yes." So the kindergartners reached into their DNA and found the gene for territoriality. They set up fences and dug trenches and fortified their positions. If the origin of the hostilities were obscure, the point of the game became increasingly clear: the last man standing.

Children all over the country were shaken by the image of the Twin Towers collapsing. They absorbed the fear, shock and grief of the adults around them, as well as the enormity of fallen buildings, smoldering wreckages, and sudden irrevocable death. It changed the way they walked in the world. Many schools brought in counselors to work with the children, or to advise the teachers about how to deal with all the attendant emotions this tragedy created. Then the country held its breath. The desire for vengeance was palpable. War was inevitable. Anna Freud and Dorothy Burlingham wrote about the effects of war on children. Although their observations were written in 1942 and based on children who physically experienced war, who played "joyfully on bombed sites, around bomb craters," I believe their insights are applicable to all children who experience war, however indirectly. "The danger lies in the fact that the destruction raging in the outer world may meet the very real aggressiveness which rages in the inside of the child. At the age when education should start to deal with these impulses, confirmation should not be given from the outside world that the same impulses are uppermost in other people."

Surviving war physically, let alone psychologically is the immediate problem for many of the world's children. Shortly after the United States went to war against Afghanistan, an old friend called me. She had opposed the Vietnam war and the Gulf war, but she called to inform me that she supported this war because "They (the terrorists) killed babies, Sue." But my friend didn't call when the picture of a little, Afghan girl of six, wearing her lovely green party dress, was on the front page of all the newspapers— a victim of a U.S. bomb gone wrong. Derrill Bodley and Rita Lasar, both of whom lost family members on September 11, traveled to Afghanistan to bring attention to the civilian casualties. While there, Bodley met with Abdul Basier, whose five-year old daughter was killed by a U.S. bomb that missed its target. I want to believe that my friend, even though she did not call me, was touched by Bodley's sparse but essential words: "This man has lost what I have lost. We are no different." The Unicef State of the World's Children 2001 reports that as a result of war, "In the past decade 2 million children have been killed, 4 to 5 million disabled, 1 million orphaned and 12 million left homeless." It's unfortunate that we can't really absorb numbers this big, or see these children as our own children or grandchildren; we would be calling one another all the time.

But morality is a luxury. My grandson's ability to weep for the smashed spider, to choose vegetarianism, to move his plastic soldiers from one trench to the next with no physical or invisible psychological repercussions stems from the fact that the children in the United States are in a kind of aristocracy in relationship to many of the world's children. Some children are not playing—they actually are soldiers. Writing for the American Friends Service Committee, Shannon McManimon writes that there are "approximately 300,000 children under 18 . . . most child soldiers are from 15 to 17 years old but others are as young as 7. These children often start out acting as porters, cooks, spies, or sexual slaves." Because violence has become a way of life for these child soldiers, as Anna Freud and Dorothy Burlingham pointed out, the children have severe problems readjusting to community life.

I love the idea of protecting children whether from cluster bombs or violent images on TV. I admire countries like Norway, Sweden and Canada for taking *Mighty Morphin Power Rangers* and *Teenage Mutant Ninja Turtles* off of the air because they concluded they were too violent for children. For years it was argued that you could not incontrovertibly prove the connection between smoking and cancer. How many cumulative studies, how many copycat crimes do we need before we protect our children from the inundation of violence in our culture? If in the nature vs. nurture argument E.O. Wilson comes down on the side of the inheritability of aggressive instincts, he also goes to great lengths to stress the importance of culture. "We know that virtually all of human behavior is transmitted by culture." Like family, church, and school, TV is a major cultural transmitter. Unfortunately, most of us have no input regarding the content of this powerful tool; we can only turn it on, or turn it off.

I was pleased to hear that the elementary school my grandson attends has adopted a plan called Peacebuilders. The stated purpose of the Peacebuilder Plan is "to create a vision in children's minds about the benefits of increasing the peace. ...It serves as a model of how kids can affect their world to achieve positive ends, even when they might believe that's not possible." The blue and green symbol of the earth dots the page on which the Peacebuilder's pledge appears. Each morning after the Pledge of Allegiance, my grandson says: "I am a Peacebuilder. I pledge to praise people, to give up put-downs, to seek wise people, to notice and speak up about hurts I have caused, and to right wrongs. I will build peace at home, at school and in my community each day." It's a lovely vision, but have you noticed that we rarely talk about peace anymore? The author Lawrence Durrell wrote, somewhere in the *Alexandrian Quartet*, that the Greeks had invented the idea of the soul in the mad hope that it might take, perhaps Peacebuilders is an attempt to reinvent the idea of a world without war.

There is some research to support the idea that a community's values, if faithfully conveyed, can derail the aggressive instincts woven into our genetic material. Among "the tiny minority" of peaceful societies, Wilson cites the Semai of Malay. He says the Semai can't even imagine violent aggression. "Murder is unknown, no explicit word for kill exists ('hit' is the preferred euphemism), children are not struck, and chickens are beheaded only as a much regretted necessity. Parents carefully train their children in these habits of nonviolence." Though I understand Wilson's pointed "tiny minority" to be emphasizing the fact that the overwhelming preponderance of human societies have opted for violence, I choose to seize on the possibility of choice. Wilson also writes about the Maori, who after obtaining muskets from the British colonists, almost succeeded in wiping themselves out in tribal warfare. When they realized this, however, they reshaped their culture into a peaceable one. Wilson concludes from the Maori experience that: "The full evolution of warfare can be reversed even in the face of entrenched cultural practice."

In the animal kingdom as well, there is fresh evidence that aggressive behavior can be modified. An experiment by zoologist and ethnologist Franz De Waal placed easy-going stump-tailed macaques with rhesus monkeys who are more aggressive and have fewer resources in terms of conciliation. According to De Waal, "Our question was whether we could get any of the stump-tails' gentleness to rub off on the rhesus." After five months the rhesus behavior was altered. The rhesus learned and employed a variety of conciliatory mannerisms. Even after the stump-tails had been removed and the rhesus were left to interact with them-selves, they maintained this newly acquired pacifism. "Like chemists altering the properties of a solution, we had infused a group of monkeys of one species with the social culture, of anoth-er." The logic of these examples might indicate that pacifism could be cultivated in children as well. Following this logic, the Peacebuilder's program might alter, at least metaphorically, the chemical properties of the children. But, what happened? Peacebuilder kindergartners were playing war with little plastic soldiers.

In the sixties people used to say, "What good is an encounter group in a concentration camp?" and De Waal points out that, "conflict resolution cannot be taught without attention to the social environment within which it functions." Likewise, you can't teach children to be Peacebuilders in the midst of the most mili-taristic country in the history of the world. Though the inclination is to point to violence as an aberration, to point to TV, or movies, or toys as the source of the problem, we have to look at the larg-er picture. If our country has the largest defense budget in the history of the world, and military troops stationed around the world, if throughout our history as a nation we have placed troops in other countries over 200 times to make them do what we want-ed them to do, and if President Bush has said, "These enemies (terrorists) view the entire world as a battlefield, and we must pur-sue them wherever they are," then it stands to reason that it is necessary for our government to cultivate a culture that lends itself to militaristic fervor, and to continually cultivate a pool of potential soldiers. You can't be a drug warlord without a gun, and you can't behave like an empire without a powerful military force. The truth is this country wants my grandson, and children like my grandson to play war, and to be mentally predisposed to mak-ing war.

If the devil is in the details, the U.S. has refused to support international agreements that would raise the minimum age of soldiers to 18. McManimon writes, "Recently, Pentagon officials have contended that raising the minimum by 2 years, to 17, is unacceptable . . . U.S. opposition to age 18 is also fueled by Pentagon concerns about possible interference with its domestic

recruitment practices, especially in the wake of current enlist-
ment shortfalls. The Pentagon has greatly expanded its outreach
and advertising activities for young people, including Junior-
ROTC in high schools and various other military programs for
children as young as eight." Branches of the military pay frequent
visits to the elementary schools in my local school district, includ-
ing the Peacebuilder's campus. They speak at assemblies and are
major participants in Career Days. They display uniforms,
weapons, regalia, and the children are dazzled. Only last week, I
unrolled the local newspaper and found an ad enclosed that read,
"Are you good at foreign languages?" It went on to urge the read-
er to join the navy. When the children turn on the TV there are
recruitment advertisements, and when the children go to high
school, or to college, or to look for an elusive job, the military is
there all along the way, waiting for the jobless to turn to them.

We are a culture in contradiction. Programs like Peacebuilders,
games that teach conflict resolution, and parental practices that
eschew spanking for passive restraint demonstrate a deep regard for
getting along, as well as a strong belief that pacific values can be
taught. Yet our entire superstructure derives its logic from the
idea of constant strife, inherent aggressiveness. When I purchase
him a toy gun, yet disapprove of him when he points it at some-
one, I, too, exemplify the contradiction. When my grandson's bat-
tlefield evolves into a play center, he is trying to resolve this con-
tradiction.

One point is clear: human nature is malleable. Though we
may have ancient aggressive proclivities encoded in our DNA, we
also have powerful cultural tools that can shape and sway the
societies in which we live. The world might be otherwise. Many
people believe this without realizing it. That is why they teach
their children to share, to play peacefully, to behave compassion-
ately—in the wild hope that it will take. But as long as the largest
role model for children, the United States government, is a serial
war-maker, we must not delude ourselves that we are creeping
toward peace. The recently released book, *Silent Night*, documents
the stories of the unofficial Christmas truce between opposing
forces during World War I. On Christmas Eve and Christmas Day,
the blood-mud-and-death-weary soldiers in the trenches—not the
officers—initiated an unofficial cease-fire by exchanging little gifts
of tobacco, food, and clothing on Christmas Eve. And on
Christmas Day they wanted to play soccer, not war.

Nadia Mandilawi

1991

Yellow ribbons nailed to every tree were all I saw that summer—from the grubby bus window on the way to school. Forced to repeat Algebra because of an "F," I saw ribbons: bouncing from sweaters on women, snug around their hips, when they walked down Pearl. Each outfit planned, the ribbon carefully matched with sandals or tight pants. They passed each other in the sun and smiled with their poodles, yellow collars around the dogs, too. Those women, winking hi to one another and shaking their asses. Shiny thin ribbons, looped wide at the top and evenly cut, delicate like a corsage, deep yellow and blinding. People threw eggs and trash in our front yard, and my father couldn't explain why. *Why here? Why did they kill his roses? Why couldn't my little sister sleep at night?* He just shook his head and said it was worse in Iraq. "Things are better here," he told me, through clenched teeth. Branded at school, because I refused to wear one, I spent July with no air conditioner, my legs sticking to the plastic orange chair, *Kim loves Jake* carved in a desk, and I just sort of rolled my eyes, said the whole thing was stupid. Chad, the greaseball who sat in the back row, made me my own ribbon, wrote *terrorist bitch* in red and pinned it on my back. Parents sneered at me from station wagons in the parking lot, pointy-faced just like their damn kids. Ribbons on the freeway when we drove up to Oceanside for a weekend that summer. A row of them stapled to the wall of that salt-water taffy store by the pier. My sister and I ran up and down the beach wearing our favorite jelly shoes, avoiding the eyes of marines as they passed. Iraq on the television after we finished dinner, my father shook his head in annoyance. Reporters spiked their heels into the sand and tried to gain control of their hair as it fiercely blew in the wind. My father, sprawled in his chair, was still glaring at the television. Unable to stop myself, I called him a "sell-out" and was sent upstairs. Forced to wear a ribbon after the school phoned the house. Frayed strip around my neck. Tight knot at the nape. I did everything wrong that year. Scolded for throwing the ribbon on the kitchen counter, I had to wear it at the house too. "This is where we're from now," my father blared, towering over me, and stuck one on the collar of my dress. Yellow ribbon gnawing at me. Going for the gut and winning.

Harold Jaffe

Things To Do During Time of War (2003)

Thursday, six-fifty a.m.
Clock-radio.
Wakened out of a dream.
Your father—long dead—is in it, and you as a child.
Also a blue guitar, or maybe a banjo.
You suppress the dream, shuffle to the machine.
Access email.
104 messages, 97 of them SPAM.
(You even installed an anti-SPAM filter).
Delete SPAM.
Post an email message.
Post another.
Post another.
Send a fax.
Consult electronic address book.
Send another fax.
Shuffle into the kitchen.
Switch on the miniature kitchen TV.
Stock quotations from major markets worldwide.
Charts, graphs, visuals.
Experts' commentary.
Part and parcel of the global economy.
Does global mean totalitarian?
It would be cynical to think "yes."
Well, cynics sit at their computers and go to the bathroom.
They have mothers and fathers like everyone else.
Grind your beans.
Brewing coffee.
Add vanilla.
Designer coffee, low-carb toast, buttered.
They claim now that fat's all right.
Swallow your vitamin packet with papaya juice.
Good for digestion.
Switch off the TV.
Coffee refill.
Carry the mug of coffee to your machine.
Delete SPAM.
Asleep, awake, it multiplies like cancer.
Post another email message.
Scan pertinent web sites.
Check the weather online.

Heat, smog.
What else can it be?
Scan the *LA Times* online.
The wars they are a-spreading.
Disclosure of torture in international prisons.
Americans no less.
The business sector is booming.
Investments up, dollar steady, unemployment rising.
No, it's *employment* that is rising.
Sorry about that.
War insures investment hence insures the peace.
Afghanistan, Pakistan, Iraq, Palestine, Saudi Arabia, Syria, the
Koreas, Indonesia, Horn of Africa, Sudan, Yemen, Colombia,
Venezuela, Cuba ...
What's the deal with Cuba?
Cuba post-millennium encourages foreign investment.
With all of its setbacks, it's still a fairy tale Caribbean isle with
much to offer in the tourist sectors especially.
Born-again Cuban capitalists shuffle their feet, smoke restlessly
in the wings, waiting for Fidel to finally croak.
Neither the FBI nor the CIA could off him, but now his beard
has turned white.
Dude has to drop dead sometime.
Scan the *LA Times* sports section online: cheerleading, skate-
boarding, water-skiing, water-skateboarding, bungee jumping,
shark hunting with sharpened dildos, beach volleyball, bowling
for fat people, "world series of poker" from Las Vegas, midgets
racing monster trucks, French-kissing piranha, extreme suicide...
Fiercely competitive, every one of them.
Sip your coffee.
Exit email.
Put your machine to sleep.
Shower, shave, floss, brush, apply cologne, insert contacts.
Boxers, white tee, socks, shirt, tie, suit, shoes.
Wallet, keys, cellphone, American flag lapel pin, ID nametag,
black leather briefcase.
Clip the nametag to your lapel.
Out of the condo, into the garage.
Into your new white SUV.
Set your briefcase on the passenger seat.
Your new SUV is white like the winning side in the ongoing war
against terrorism.
Ongoing because the war will not cease until the white hats
impose their will.
Such is the price of democracy.

Smell the spanking-new leather upholstery of your new SUV.
Open the garage door with your remote.
Start the potent, sweet engine and the radio comes on.
Today, it turns out, is Orange Alert day.
So declares your Attorney General.
Al-Qaeda operatives with identical black mustaches and explo-
sives taped to their bodies have slipped across the borders.
Likely through Mexico.
Report any and all suspicious humans.
Turn off the radio and insert a CD.
Hook your cellphone on the dash.
Turn on the A.C.
Off to the office.
Receive a call on your cell in your white SUV.
Make a call on your cell in your white SUV.
Consult your electronic phone book.
Make another call.
Accelerate to 80.
Coasting.
Speed kills, but not in your white SUV.
Rides like a sharp knife cutting through butter.
Change lanes on the freeway.
Mutter at the other drivers.
Mentally compare other SUVs on the freeway with your own.
Fast-forward the CD.
A swarthy subhuman with a black mustache pulls alongside
you in his black Citroën sedan, makes agitated gestures, then
lowers his window and shoots you in the head with his Beretta
semi-automatic.
You're dead so you don't make it to the office.
Actually you don't die, you aren't shot, you make it to the office.
Turn into the underground lot.
Park in your middle manager slot.
Turn off the A.C.
Employ your secure ID to enter the building.
Employ your secure ID to enter your sector.
In your office you set your black briefcase on your desk.
Framed photo of your adolescent daughter from your divorced
marriage on your desk.
Girl's name is Holly.
Divorced wife's name is **money-lust demon from the nether
regions.**
Inventory the messages on your office phone.
Inventory the nine faxes, six of them SPAM.
Remove your suit jacket and hang it on the coat hanger.

Your next promotion will mean a larger office and small closet to hang your suit jacket in.

If you're lucky.

Move to the computer terminal alongside your desk and access your email.

119 messages, 103 of them SPAM.

Delete the SPAM.

Post eleven messages.

Send three faxes.

Make six phone calls from your cell while sitting at the terminal.

Access CNN news online.

Another suicide bombing, another helicopter gunship attack, more torture uncovered, another savage beheading, oil prices rising steeply thanks to the Arab oil cartel.

Orange Alert will continue at least through the weekend.

Send for coffee, double latte from Starbucks.

Phone buzzes, meeting at eleven in the boardroom.

Latte arrives.

More phone and online business.

At the meeting a VP with a bad hair weave addresses the managers.

Earnings are up this quarter but they could do better, must do better.

Or else.

"Or else" implied not spoken.

Not unlike the official orders to "interrogate with firmness."

Sanitized way of saying "torture the gooks."

The army reserve drones called up to serve in Iraq prisons understand.

The national guard drones called up to serve in Iraq prisons understand.

After the boardroom meeting, a hurried buffet lunch in the cafeteria downstairs.

Back at the office, more calls, online contacts, faxes, another meeting, more coffee.

Decaf this time.

You're back in the white SUV, on the freeway, 5:40 pm, gridlock.

Receiving calls, making calls, switching lanes, muttering at other drivers.

A swarthy subhuman with a black mustache pulls alongside you in his black Citroën sedan, makes agitated gestures, then lowers his window and shoots you in the head with his Beretta semi-automatic.

This time you do die.

Nonetheless you return to your condo at 6:40, pull into the

garage.

Inside at your computer are 111 messages, 103 of them SPAM.

Eight faxes, six of them SPAM

Seven-twenty p.m.

Enema time.

Warm water, not hot.

Mix with a teaspoon of chamomile tea.

Spruce Street Bridge

Photo by yukimi levas-anderson

WHERE WE LIVE NOW

Marilyn Chin
Where We Live Now (Vol. 3, #4)
eternal noonscape

I don't love you for your savage beauty
not for your pale fragrant flesh,
not for your sun-spectred countenance
and your stars that paralyze the sky,
not for your silver-timbred limbs scarred
by a thousand axes. I yearn for
all you can give me, the wild geese
that wing over the moon blindly.
The white egret on a dunghill stands
on ceremony, on one thin leg,
calling her mate: hello, hello,
we have had a bad connection
since Ma Bell shattered—
cicadas chivvy in the rosemary,
blue jays wreak havoc
on the wires—the frogs in the pond
mock the ocean and its depth:
they cannot know their limitations.
Jacarandas wave their purple dare.
Lush lantana cannot hide
the local banal geckos; the sun sets
on the frontier Korean grass;
at the Aztec watering hole
horses, motorcycles, dump trucks neigh
to the moon; paisley, dizzy succulents,
slipshod hillside robes
expose gray, bruised thighs of the barrio;
large blooms of oleander, star jasmine;
scentless forsythia brilliant yellow.
Vacuous verbena, red hibiscus dance around
the Great Mother's wide helm,
mouthing the earth's gaping hollows.

————

A jumbo jet careens between the sun and moon—
a small man controls her destiny,
veers into the vast blue loneliness.
Hello, hello, won't you call me from San Francisco,
Tel Aviv, Hong Kong, Canton, Ohio,

from your corporate e-mail address,
from your turbid moods and peccadilloes?
Won't you ring me from the netherside
of the universe, from the back entry
of Eido, . . . where the moonscape appears friendly
and truth is not a liability.
Home is the grandest illusion: Papa's
failed restaurants, Mama's broken wren
of a neck in the nest's warm alcove.
Will the thundering bring new rain?
Will I rise again and again
to greet the sun's bright welcome?
Or will it be another sleepless night
of Prozac and Yo-Yo Ma's morbiferous cello?
Alone, without you, without you,
in the Southern California morass—
arrogance, ignorance, indifference,
wave after wave the clean hubbub of freeway
delivering me, delivering me
from nowhere to nowhere, the landscape
murmuring between waking and slumber.
Lover, I am calling you
from the southernmost hinterlands,
I am scrawling a long love plume
mocking my own befuddlement.
Crows and wood doves loiter,
orange proroguing trumpet flowers
irradiated and gargantuan,
loose liana creeping up the rectum of a wall.
Hummingbirds drink
from my sanguinary confections
(preferring fiction over truth)
in plastic, vulval-red flowers.
O how their small bodies suspend,
a brilliant trapeze of the soul.
O my little winging bee-bird,
O my beauteous formula,
O Bird, O Bard—how I object
to this feeble corollary!
As you sip this perfect concoction
from my inner brown thigh,
perhaps the creatures will make peace
with these human contusions.
Perhaps Art doesn't matter—
only happiness, an eternal noonscape

more substance than shadow.
Your limp arm draped over my pillow,
the morning sun kissing it so.

————

O let the bees make honey from an iron sleeve,
let the grille beneath the house
be their sanctuary. But the wasps
that bear no honey, I have scheduled
Tuesday for their extermination.
Hello, hello, yo! Baby, Odysseus!
Will you return from your ten-year exile?
Could you love me again
in our quiet domesticity?
Penelope Wong's been waiting with her sad kohl eyes.
Could we mend the fissures in the bowl?
Meanwhile, the ocean roars against the shoals,
twenty miles of La Jolla where
the rich whites live; where sandpipers dance,
their tiny, skittery legs
foraging, pecking, never ceasing.
Another hateful colleague, another disturbing ritual
defines me—that static calamity
spreading from home to divorced home,
welling up, attempting to break
my contemplation:
             my skinhead neighbor says
that he believes in segregation,
in racial purity, *HITLER ELIMINATED THE JEWS*
FOR REASONS OF OVERPOPULATION—IT WAS
BEFORE THE PILL, HA-HA . . . IN 1955,
WEBSTER'S NEW WORLD DICTIONARY *CITES 'A RACIST'*
AS "ONE WHO IS PROUD OF ONE'S RACE."
The devil is bronze and he, too, is the flesh of God.
He went on, that little fatherfucker,
blondly in his monster truck,
that barbarian drone, that hard-metal music.
Once, I paid him fifty dollars
for pruning my exuberant loquats;
the muse extravagant by nature,
self-appointed enigma,
Minister Plenipotentiary to the Holy See,
with her ambiguous smile and silent condescension,

deigns to immortalize him here.

————

It may be plausible to assert that
phenomena have explanations,
or in the layman's terms,
they have causes.
In the picture window I yell,
Move it, El Grosso, move it.
He thinks I am saying,
Hello, lover, hello.

Zenfully, zenfully,
he drove northward, gun rack
rattling through blue void.

> *Zenfully, northward*
> *gun rack rattling*
> *blue void*

> *zenfully*
> *gunrack   rattling*
> *blue void*

> *gun rack*

> *blue*

> *void*

When my mother painted bamboo
    She saw bamboo and not herself.
Gladly, she left her body.
    Her body hardened into bamboo.
A fresh breeze made her sing;
    And she stood, singing,

One with the forest.

When / my / mother / painted / bamboo /
She / saw / bamboo / and / not / herself /
Gladly / she / left / her / body /
Her / body / hardened / into / bamboo /
A / fresh / breeze / made / her / sing /
And / she / stood / singing/
One / with / the / forest /

Hello, hello,
You had better listen to your moral thoughts,
Ms. Lookeast, Ms. Lookeast,
your mother is the right hand of Buddha,
you're more like the left hand of darkness,
snot-nosed, tousle-haired;
a persistent 5 o'clock shadow's
not very comely on a Chinese American woman.
In deep drought, knowledge does not hold water.
I'm slothful, sleepy,
no energy to divert the rivers.
The palm tree sheds a mess near my boudoir.
The rats make remorseful love in the sheaves.
The local flora's invaded by exotic seedlings;
cacti mixed with imperial cherries, mixed
with woodsy wildflowers, mixed
with cheap bareroot roses from "Home Depot."

———

A Chink has moved into their neighborhood
and there's nothing they can do about it.
A hawk tarries, and the wind chimes call
infrequently: this exile, this malaise,
this complacency. In this motherless desert heat
I am missing you. Welcome, sweet sojourner,
welcome to Chin's promontory.
No giant statue of Buddha or gilded pagoda
carved in mist; no Mao's Yenan caves
deep in the rhapsody of revolution.
No majestic Gueilin, no silk route to enlightenment,
no "Red Detachment of Women"—jaded scabbards, piqued bayonets,
pirouette, arabesque, changez, changez into the distance—

but a view of the freeway and the borderlands:
California's best kept secret. You said,
Your ass, your beautiful ass fascinates me.
So, the birds chirp *ming ming,*
and the dogs bark *hung, hung.*
A gingko traveled ten thousand miles from her homeland
to become a weed tree in the new kingdom,
and another blight cracks through the groundswell.
I wear a watch to bed to remind myself
of my own dying. I nail a calendar on the wall
so that each day shall pass in vain.
Come back, come back, my soul, I summon you,
come back to San Diego. The sun's so hot
we can fry an egg on the blacktop
and make soap with the lye.

Chicano Park #1

Photo by yukimi levas-anderson

Leilani Clark

Fear in the Heart of Golden Hill

Ten years ago, the main business stretch of Golden Hill along 25th Street contained liquor stores, the closed down Turf Club, Kentucky Fried Chicken, Mexican eateries and Panchita's, a popular bakery that serves everything from empanadas to elaborately decorated birthday cakes. After the re-opening of the Turf Club in 1996 by the owner of the local rock club The Casbah, interest and growth in this area surged as local hipsters discovered a watering hole that gave them a place to see and be seen. Although this particular enclave of San Diego had previously been off-limits for most middle-class artist types because of rumors of crime and violence, a transition began to occur as hipsters, artists and musicians started flocking into the working-class Latino neighborhood.

A few years down the line, Krakatoa Café was established directly next door to the Turf Club, and in January of 2004 remodeling began on a gallery space across the street from the two flourishing businesses. The new owners gutted the remains of the preceding business, a rundown Mexican curio shop, but the etched sign advertising "Regalos y Novedades" remained even after the building had been repainted in bright, artsy reds. According to an article in *Fahrenheit* magazine, the owners were drawn to the location because it was near their favorite businesses and it catered to a dream of establishing a more New York-style atmosphere in San Diego. Small mention was made of the original, mainly working-class Latino community that maintains a strong presence in Golden Hill despite rising housing costs. The goal of the gallery was to be an anchor in a triangle of businesses in Golden Hill providing victuals and libations to the bohemians and increasing numbers of yuppies who were drawn to the gentrified atmosphere of Golden Hill. Similar to the "transformed" Brooklyn borough of Williamsburg, which went from Hasidic to hedonistic, people could walk within a few blocks to have a drink and catch a gallery show.

This dream, however naïve, was shattered on a cold night in mid-March. In the midst of an opening for an art exhibit featuring graffiti inspired work, the gallery was bum rushed by a group of approximately ten teenagers. The kids walked off with a $6,000 painting by Los Angeles artist Meir 1. When gallery owners chased the group, entering into a potentially high-danger situation of three against ten, chaos ensued. After being hit over the head with a forty-ounce bottle, one owner ended up in the hospital with skull contusions. Another hid under a car as the youths pelted him with glass. The painting was not recovered.

After only one day of deliberation the owners made the decision to close the gallery. Financial repercussions of the violent assault were cited as the main reason for the closure. Unfortunately, the hospitalized co-owner did not have health insurance and had amassed a small fortune in bills. In addition, the other two owners were plagued by fears that something of this nature would happen again if they did not close immediately. Later, one of the gallery owners told a local paper that they wanted to reopen in the future but preferably in an area like La Jolla or Del Mar, where they might be more accepted.

As an employee of the café directly across the street, I watched the space develop and grew excited about its potential for contributing a positive, artistic anchor to the community. After-school arts programs along with the workshops and shows featuring local artists were on the planning board. The assault threatened the dream, and fear put the nail through the coffin. But that fear goes further than just a reaction to the stupidity of a group of drunken teens.

It is easy to espouse liberal ideas about diversity and inclusion in the insulated circle of an alternative creative community, but the reality is that there is still rampant misjudgment and alienation of the "other" within such groups. The slapdash closing of the gallery did not stem solely from the fear of another assault. In actuality, it is fear of the neighborhood, fear of the teenagers who come from backgrounds unlike their own, a gap that the gallery owners made no attempt to bridge.

San Diego is a place rife with segregation. Unlike cities such as New York and Chicago, there is little commingling of races. Hence, the racial fear of the "other" is an unfortunate reality in America's Finest City. It is called white flight—running from a place because it is perceived as a source of danger and violence; running from something that is not understood. Instead of facing up to the challenge, joining the community, becoming a source of inspiration and artistic empowerment, it is easier to retreat back into safe, comfort zones like the whitest of all enclaves, La Jolla.

From what source do such fears truly rise? In the twenty-first century it can be difficult for people, especially those coming out of artistic and "politically-savvy" communities, to fess up to underlying problems of race and class in their own lives, in their own neighborhoods. This is an issue that is rarely discussed in the "San Diego scene," most likely because the city still remains so segregated that it is easy for people to pretend that the tension does not exist. Yet, if gentrification continues at its current pro-lific rate, these issues must be addressed. The only other option is displacing the communities that are being gentrified by the influx of young urban types and bohemians who do not want to deal with inherent issues of race and class as they colonize these neighborhoods.

Who were these gallery owners so scared of? Why did they feel targeted? This fear is tinged with more than just a fear of violence. It is a fear of an entire culture. Perhaps it comes from the realization that Golden Hill is not the completely gentrified enclave that they had assumed it to be. Is it that the neighbor-hood was not as truly de-browned as they hoped it would be? The youth were described as local gangster types. Kids in khakis, chinos and white t-shirts, possibly a group of brown kids, maybe Mexican, Chicano. It makes one wonder, if this had been a group of white kids, would the gallery owners have been so quick to run? Seemingly, their inability to understand where the incident might have come from was a factor in the decision to close. Why not examine the community? Examine the inci-dences of violence? Fight the fear through knowledge of the community? The incidents that led up to the assault on the gallery show a remarkable lack of street smarts that could have kept this from happening, or taken it down to a much less dam-aging level.

In times of transition, it's easy to end up standing on shaky ground. The gentrification of San Diego neighborhoods such as Golden Hill is an example of the way that underlying issues of race and class, that are not addressed by those rushing to estab-lish themselves in these neighborhoods, can end up blowing up. Looking across the street now, the gallery has once again become an empty space. Much like the abandoned storefronts that line my own neighborhood of Logan Heights, it is a space that held promise but now decays. But this is not a physical decay. It is a failure. I see fear of brown here-the type of generalization that has created a gap between social groups and classes for centuries, and the assumption that the crimes of one are the crimes of all. Yet, if gentrification continues at the rapid rate it is currently at in San Diego, as condominiums and swanky shops rise up around the old warehouse spaces of downtown, then those who are ben-efiting from it, or participating in the process, must consider their own biases and assumptions in terms of race and class before gal-livanting in. Are you scared? Do you feel safe only if the neighbor-hood is whitewashed, economically homogeneous, and bohemian only in building colors? It's something to consider.

Chicano Park #2

Photo by yukimi levas-anderson

Angela Boyce

Blessed

The teenaged boy
who sells tamales
door-to-door
person-to-person
creating
a fragile web of connection
via mobile eatery
ears
are replaced by oversized headphones.
Head bobbing,
bursts de la canta erupting de la boca
he stops at the waiting door
open in anticipation of a visitor
the day's coming warmth.
"Care for some homemade tamales today?"
he calls blindly into the cavern of space
cement walls still cold with night's air.
Question answers question,
"What kind you got?"
My voice a shadow in the darkness,
I beckon him in with my physical presence
as I listen to the litany of beef, chicken, cheese....
I'd hoped for sweet, settle for chicken.
Two dollar bills pressed into his palm as I ask,
"How's your day been so far?"
Figuring... assuming... knowing
it's been an early morning rising
hot steam and corn flour
beef chicken cheese
a cooler on a cart
the homeless one without enough change in his needy palm
a steady question and a smile
music and hope.
His dark brown eyes, neat combed hair
oversized jeans and polo shirt speak volumes
but the answer comes unexpected.
"Blessed."
One word for the obvious.
We are living.... Just enough for the city.
Two tamales golden husks seeping grease through a paper towel
warm my hand
as the muted musica fades
and the screen door quietly shuts
and my smile makes its way to my eyes.

Photo by Hendrix Knowells

Play Downtown

reg e. gaines

Godiva's Dilemma

for the Bag Lady on Broadway & 5th

"all I was doin'
was diggin' in the garbage
and this cop asks for my ID
and I tell him
I ain't got no ID
and that's when he
starts to frisk me
and I sass him
and he pulls out his cuffs
almost breaks my wrists
and that's why cops ain't shit
I mean they not even human
they devils all of 'em
just like them Black Muslims say
just like *louis farakhan say*—
...but he killed *Him*
you know he did
talking about how he
helped to create the climate
but it was winter anyway
so why they had to be so cold
followin' *Him* around
in that broke down car
jumpin' out
when *He* stop at the light
dime store lawyer
layin' low in the back
tryin' to play with them
jewboy bigwigs
that's why they threw Him out
talkin' bout
He burnt it down himself
but you know yuseff did that
cuz ain't no nigga
gonna be standin
in front of no burnin' house
fifteen degrees
with a rifle in *His* hand
standin' there in His underwear
'cuz I could sure put on a better show than that!'

cuz see
if you want to be in the limelight
you got to get some shades
cuz niggas is shadey as shit
but then there's more to life
than bowties and beanpies
there's pumpkin pie
sweet potato pie
peach cobbler see...
niggers don't eat no apple pie
especially a la mode
that's when they put
vanilla ice cream on it
then it melt and get all soggy
and who wanna eat that soggy shit
soggy like saggin' like flat
like them flat ass whitegirls
and why a brother
wanna fuck somethin'
ain't got no ass
be like ridin' a bicycle
ain't got no seat
cuz all I was doin'
was mindin' my busines
lookin' in the garbage
for somethin' to eat—
now they takin' my
black ass to jail..."

Sharon Elise

The sun rose again

The sun rose again, sent shimmers across waves
That crested and washed the debris of shells and bottles
And old beach gear upon the sand
Spread flat and damp below treacherous
Cliffs that chip in chunks, send squirrels flying
Mansion dwellers shooting concrete pilings
Down to solid ground 8 stories below homes
Look down across the beach and out to the pacific
Lean into wind and away from the highway
Where tourists and valley visitors, surfers and muscled cyclists,
Old men with dogs, power walkers goose stepping to cds,
Runners indecent in open flapped trunks
Stream in both directions
Past cafes and coffee shops, thrift stores and boutiques,
Restaurants with patios open to splashing waves and seagulls
Where clerks and waitresses snub the clientele to show
How little they need them and their money, spent freely
While Mexican busboys and gardeners and maids keep
It all clean for such little money they live
Crowded in two bedroom duplexes, spilling out into driveways
Crammed with fix it yourself cuz you don't have the money
And make it yourself cuz you don't have the money projects
Neighborhoods packed and temporary between mansions
Springing up stucco and spreading high and wide for
Panoramic ocean views
In a place where some people just don't see each other
See each other, see each other
Even in the democracy of grocery store lines where
Inequality lies in the gaze and hello shared or not and with whom
Even clerks save smiles and little "what a day I've had" gossip
For people who speak English, haven't bothered to learn or won't
Use a little como esta ustedes? And que bonita la niña!
Or meet the open dark eyes with a smile,
These are not "beach people," (who were always black and brown)
Those are designated by bleached blond hair and skin that reddens and
Cracks in the sun, these are those others who live on other streets in
Crowded homes, whose women walk clusters of children, hands linked
To school and from school, pushing a stroller with old wobbly tires,
Wearing slippers and scarves and shawls, their bodies covered
Contrast to the business suits and tennis outfits of soccer moms.
These are not the children who come to the park to play, or

Spend the night with friends, or gossip on the computer chat line.
They will meet later in my college classroom and they still will not speak
Or smile, will not choose any other for group projects,
For life will stay strangers under the same shimmering sun, lives
Eroding and chipping away in chunks, spilling down the cliff to the
ocean floor.

minerva

The Original Negro Blondes

I'll need them all in my old age.
The original Negro blondes
and strong broads.
If only to remind me
that it's just not true
sometimes.

Folk say, "You black women
are so strong. Won't you be
my neighbor?"
For thirty years, I bow
shuffle, accept, and thank.
Thirty-first year, no dice.

How do people know this?
Why do they think that?
Tell me how many of us you know.
Is it just Channel whatever Mollie
or maybe even me?

You don't see us when we cry.
Is this about Halle Berry?
What about Etta James?
Rage to Survive
is the title of her story.

Round light face
graces the book cover.
Etta James.
The original Negro blonde?
Now her head is full
of black hair and age.

Face swollen
from takin' it
on the chin
continues to swell
right in front of me.

Beauty in song.
"I'd rather go blind,"

she sang.
Etta James!
The original Negro blonde.

Yes, Josephine Baker.
Yes, Dorothy Dandridge.
We hear beauty in their blonde pain.
Pain in their beauty.

Etta's pain seems just plain beauty.
Listen to her!
My original Negro blonde
and strong broad.
See her face
and you'll see you or even me.

No, I'm not Dorothy,
or Etta or Billie or blonde.
Just thinking and writing and tired
of the strong black woman experience.
So, I hear Etta James
as strength and prayer.

Yes, she's right here in my head.
Etta James.
The original Negro blonde
and sometimes strong broad.
As many of my sisters are these days.
I'll need them all in my old age.

Megan Pincus Kajitani

Can't a Woman Just Be Naked in Peace?

I'm a liberal woman of the new millennium, I'm comfortable with my body, I love nature, I hate tan lines, and I'm trying to get to know my new home down the coast here in San Diego. So what else to do on a beautiful Friday afternoon but throw a book and a towel in my old beach bag and hit the nude side of Black's?

Now, I've done topless beaches in Europe, where nobody looks twice. I assumed the famed Black's Beach would be similarly sophisticated—an earthy place with an appreciation for the freedom of the human form, in all of its permutations—similarly, "it's just a body, get over it."

So, I head down the long, dusty, cliffside pathway to Black's and waltz (to the right of the orange cones) past the birthday-suited sun worshippers dotting the sand. I look around, smile with relief, and think, "How fabulous. Right here in San Diego, our own little commune of open-minded folks, comfortable with their regular, protruding bodies amidst a tight-assed, silicone-implanted coast. *And* no tan lines!"

Then, as I walk a bit farther, a little flutter in my gut notifies me that there are many more men than women hanging out in their bare nakedness here. It's that flutter in my gut that says to keep my wits about me, the flutter we women often experience when we find ourselves outnumbered by the Y chromosomes.

Brushing off the flutter (as we also often do, being a culture of women raised with the "disease to please" or what I like to call the "Just Smile Virus"), I forge on with my liberated woman adventure. Continuing down the beach to a somewhat secluded spot, I lay out my towel about 20 feet behind a male-female middle-aged couple tossing a Frisbee (they seem safe enough), near a pile of rocks shaped like a seal balancing a ball on its nose.

I strip off my confining bikini, take a long, deep breath, and soak in the moment, the encompassing sun, the freedom of being on this stunning, cliff-framed beach in all my naturalness, reveling in my independence, counting my blessings for this place of beauty and acceptance. After a few minutes, I start to read, relax, dig my toes into the sand. Then, the flutter calls again.

I look up, and behind me, along the cliffs, two naked men have appeared, each alone. One walks very slowly, back and forth. The other sits his bare butt on a rock about 15 feet away to my left. Both guys seem to be staring at me, both seem a little creepy. "Oh, stop imagining things," I tell myself. "It's a nude beach. It's just a different experience. You're being paranoid."

I shake it off and continue to read my book—well, sort of. I'm feeling a little less liberated and peaceful now, a little more naked and alone all of a sudden. Another dude appears, throwing out a blanket behind me on the other side, looking at me, too. I try to ignore them all, mind my own business, don't feel intimidated, don't allow my freedom to be disturbed. Then, I think, "Maybe they're just doing their own thing, why do I think they're looking at me?" Or maybe I should just enjoy the experience of people comfortable enough to look at each other's bodies, of men appreciating my wonderfully imperfect body in a town where Barbie bodies are the gold standard. I try to rationalize. But the flutter won't go away. No matter how much I try to convince myself to "just smile," it doesn't feel good. The flutter is turning into a mild internal panic.

Just then, like an angel appearing for Jesus or Glinda the Good Witch for Dorothy, the woman from the Frisbee couple walks over to me. I look up at her, in her shining tan skin, and she smiles. "Are you new here?" she asks me. I tell her I am. She says her name is Elaine, and she and her husband are members of a group called the Black's Beach Bares.

She asks me if I noticed the men gathering behind me. I tell her I did. The Bares, she says, try to keep single women (any women) on the beach safe from these looky-loos, guys who aren't on the beach just to enjoy the natural beauty, but to leer at it, or treat it like a kinky sex show.

Elaine, her husband, and other good-spirited people who want Black's to remain free and comfortable for women (and anybody), patrol the beach, offering strategically placed umbrellas to women or couples, any vulnerable souls who want shielding from these nasty dogs. The Bares always congregate around that rock shaped like a seal balancing a ball on its nose. *(Got that, ladies? If you go alone to Black's, sit near the seal rock.)*

Guardian Angel Elaine invites me to move my towel closer to her and her husband. I do, and within minutes, the cliffhangers are dust. She turns to me and says, "See, that's all it takes. We don't let them get away with it." Right on, Elaine. She and her husband, upstanding members of the Black's Beach Bares, nod and smile at me, then go back to their private conversation.

I sit on my relocated towel and try to read a while longer. I want to stay there and not leave, just to say to them all, "I have the freedom to be here." But, I must admit, the mood is lost. My elation and titillation with this gorgeous nude beach have fizzled to a bit of the "ick." It's the "ick" that comes when leering guys suddenly turn feeling sexy and liberated into feeling exposed, vulnerable, like a dirty vulture's dinner prey.

I pack up in a few minutes, say a friendly farewell to my unexpected protectors, tie on my bikini and head back up the beach. Several nude men wading in the shallow surf smile at me and say hello as I walk back toward the orange cones. I don't know whether to respond. I decide not to. It's sad.

This beach, with its gold-speckled sand, cresting waves, and towering cliffs could not be more beautiful, just like a naked body in its splendor and comfort. But I'm not sure I feel safe here now. The Black's Beach Bares do an amazing service for women (couples, families, anyone) who want to enjoy this beach. But I'm so disheartened that they must exist. That our public culture forces nakedness and solo females to be constantly self-conscious and even in danger.

I head over to the other side of Black's, spend the rest of my afternoon laying out (avec bathing suit), watching the surfing, having a pleasant chat with a couple of friendly Aussies, reading my book. It's a nice time, but I can't help feeling a little heavy-hearted the rest of the day. On the bright side was a new experience, a day at this unique San Diego gathering place with myself, and an enlightened, socially-conscious group of people who made it possible. On the dark side was the flutter, the "ick," the deep-seated knowledge that being a woman trying to do anything alone in the world today means being forever cautious. Freedom with limits. But, in the end, I suppose, freedom nonetheless. And freedom is usually hard won.

So, I won't let the looky-loos ruin fabulous Black's Beach. I'll go back, maybe with a friend next time, and I'll help fight for the right to be safe and comfortable. I won't smile when I'm being leered at; I'll tell those bastards to move along and let me read. And I'll thank my lucky stars for the Black's Beach Bares, who help make our world, and San Diego, a place where a woman like me can continue my quest for liberation, joy, adventure, equality, and, damn it, no tan lines.

Sydney Brown

The Role of the Illegal Immigrant in the
Local Economy

In 1988, David Avalos, Louis Hock, and Elizabeth Sisco designed a poster. They paid for advertising space on one hundred local busses for one month. It was the first of seven collaborative projects meant to draw attention to the treatment of illegal immigrants in the city bordering Mexico-San Diego.

San Diego was in the "glare of the national media" preparing for the Super Bowl.

The poster looks like this (from left to right, a montage): Nonwhite hands scraping white plate with food that looks like vomit, nonwhite hands in silvery handcuffs, a policeman's gun, a hotel doorknob sign for "Maid Service Please," a nonwhite hand opening that door. Across the top and on the bottom, white block letters state: "Welcome to America's Finest Tourist Plantation." Did I say the photo is in black & white? It is.

One hundred posters became thousands of reproductions when front-page stories accompanied by photographs were published in the morning and evening editions of the San Diego Tribune, *as well as in the local edition of the* Los Angeles Times *on January 7, 1988. Commentaries followed: certain*

In 1988, I was waiting tables in a "Mexican" restaurant on the harbor of picturesque San Diego bay. It was called Carlos Murphy's. Basically Americanized Mexican Food—lots of cheddar cheese and sour cream and Jimmy Buffett pumped through speakers strategically placed throughout the restaurant. People liked the food and service, but we were mostly popular for our location.

I was twenty-two and sleeping with one of the illegal workers. There were many. He was our best line cook. No one knew about it. We used to pick up a twelve pack after long shifts, play "Buzz" in Spanish on the sand under the beautiful San Diego moon and stars. He taught me to count to one hundred in his language. I taught him how to fuck in mine. He taught me how to find Orion. I taught him about white women. He taught me how to watch the dark waves push into white and run up the sand.

He was a beautiful man. Dark brown eyes with gold flakes, a round hard ass, brown skin that smelled like the kitchen at work. He loved to go down on me. I never did on him, and he never asked why.

When Immigration did their

city officials let it be known to the press that they were trying to have the poster removed, and national coverage ensued. (In USA Today, the poster appeared alongside pictures of the Denver Broncos and the Washington Redskins.)

The role of the illegal immigrant in the local economy and the validity of the poster were debated through editorials and letters to the editors of the local papers.

Throughout January 1988, the poster was a catalyst for debate regarding the intersection of a pressing social issue with a complex aesthetic one—the shape of art for public spaces.

sweeps, I used to miss him. When we got busy on hot summer nights, he moved my orders in front of the other girls'.

Once when it was slow, he backed me into the dry storage room, lifted me onto a stack of boxes filled with canned meat from Venezuela, and did me right there. He stifled my moans with his hand, placed the other firmly on my ass. I never knew a man who could move like him. I remember not liking the feel of his greasy hand on my mouth and thinking my life would be over if someone needed some meat, beans, flour or something. I made him stop and block the door.

Nights I didn't work, I'd sneak him through my dark apartment after my roommates had gone to bed and then out before they left for work. He never questioned anything. On the weekends we'd sleep in my car or pass out on the beach. We never ate a meal together in a restaurant, never saw a movie, never even stayed in a hotel. Never walked through a mall or park holding hands. Never took a photo together. I have a card where he calls me his valentine. Valentine is spelled wrong.

At the company Christmas party he sat at a table with the rest of the back-of-the-house. I sat across the room. I brought a date from my English class. Eric was his name. Eric was a surfer. I called him my boyfriend. We'd met each other's mothers after three dates. Sometimes it just happens that way.

He told me I looked like he remembered our sea, "hermosa," when I slipped away from my date to meet him in one of the hotel's suites. "Las llaves," he said, "were a gift from mi hermana." She worked in the hotel. I smiled. He lifted my dress and shoved me against a print of the Coronado Bridge. For the first time, I stopped him.

"Por que mi amor?"

I said I'd been dating this guy from college and he was out in the bar and I didn't really feel— He placed his finger to my lips and kissed my cheek, "El vuelo de un escondido corazon." Then in English, he told me he needed me, loved me. In our hurry, we'd left the room dark; I could barely see him. I'd forgotten what he looked like up close. His finger smelled like the kitchen at work. I did nothing, said nothing in an instant I couldn't count. He started to unzip my dress and I motioned to keep it on, and then worked to remove his pants. I could not wait to get out of that room, quit my job—never see him again.

His name was Roberto.

Flavia Tamayo

Shoes

Maquiladora on the border. Reams
of leather. Diagonal cutter. The facing.
Curved-needle. Spindle. Thread.
Stitched by hands de las abuelas, señoras,
señoritas, niñas like loose seams pulled
taut. Patchwork of lockstitches
on sole's edge. Conversations among
workers about lovers, attaching eyelets,
weddings, baptisms, using clinching
nails to fasten the outer sole, dampness,
hunched backs. Passage of time
like creeping moss on factory wall.
Whistle sounds to end graveyard shift.
Foreman opens steel doors onto desert
moon. She takes the hour bus ride
to her small town. Bent over in her seat,
she holds her face in her hands, finds
temporary sleep. She dreams about
women walking into eternity, heels
pressed to earth. She wakes, makes
trek across desert alone, three miles
to family's plywood shack on outskirts
of town. Her black shoes ashen with dust.
Muffled footsteps pursue her. Next day,
cactus thorns found embedded in her palms,
her soles face skyward.

Painting by Mario Chacon

We Take Our Babies With Us

Mario Chacon, Paintings: Prison Series '04

A San Diego City College student named Armando Martinez inspires the three paintings in this series. Armando enrolled in classes at City College soon after a lengthy period of incarceration. Realizing that so many of his peers were incarcerated, he lamented the effects on those left behind—the suffering families, fatherless babies, grieving mothers, lonely siblings, and anguished pregnant wives.

This series of three paintings was created while Armando progressed through his first semester at City College. As the series approached completion, I was shocked to learn that a rival gang member in a drive-by shooting tragically murdered Armando.

Here I attempt to capture the poetic essence of Armando's words. He talked about how incarcerated young fathers "take their babies with them," and how in the case of a pregnant girlfriend left behind, "even the unborn" suffer. He described prison as an inescapable cage that "just goes round and round", as he painfully described the injustice in our justice system. Hence the titles of these paintings are:

1. We Take Our Babies With Us (babies crying in jail cell) 24"x30"
2. Even the Unborn (pregnant moms/incarcerated fetuses) 24"x30"
3. The Cage (four desperate men in a cage) 24"x30"

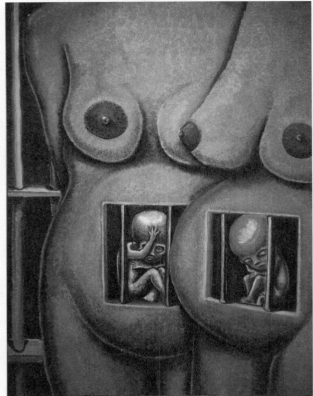

Painting by Mario Chacon

Even the Unborn

Painting by Mario Chacon

The Cage

d. zenani mzube

jahi: the revisit

he is my found poem
the words in the newspaper i
tried to disassemble for
a mistake
misunderstanding
misconstruction anything
but a mislaid toddler
i cut out clues and claims tried to ignore the clamor inside my
womb, say
he's gone girl
he's gone
little jahi is
gone

he is the free verse i cannot write if i do somebody will come
but won't knock first just barge in and confiscate my pen for threatening to
put out the crack in a
mama's
husband's
pipe
i trip
        over the step
in *father*
name his name
peep his ho card from a deck
of lost baby lies
my naked light bulb looms above fumbling fingers:
what did you do?
what did you do with little jahi?

he is my end rhyme but i can't find the word—
feigning for some fruition not another baby face on my junk mail
please
babies are not lost socks at the laundromat
they won't appear miraculously to complete the pair

out looking for you deep
inside me i knew i would
fall down
if your grays turned up
got to

keephoping
missing little jahi
it's year three
still hoping

he is my haiku 3 lines heavy
17 syllables deep
april 25th rears its rememory
in baltimore in san diego
perpetual tales of a child gone missing

would have been today
first day in preschool
except you did not answer roll
called your name
jahi turner
you did not answer

but no worries jahi
we
will hold your place
tell your mama and her husband too—
we
hold
your place
in
line

Josh Baxt

Human Resources

Jerry Johansen works flextime, seven to four, Monday through Friday and alternate Saturdays. The early mornings make him tired, but he enjoys his afternoon naps, though they don't really offer much sleep. Sometimes the noises from outside his bedroom make rest difficult. Skateboards, leaf blowers, chain saws, garbage trucks, car alarms. Jerry is sensitive to noise, but even when the world is quiet, the inner noise is just as bad. Worse. His mind works overtime, hemorrhaging imaginary scenarios that make him roll around or coil up like a snake. He relives arguments with Elise, or composes his resignation speech or finally says yes to Anna. For many years, he pitched a perfect seventh game of the World Series and graciously signed autographs after the game. Once he spared the life of a man who'd been tailgating him. Jerry drives fast in the fast lane, but the man, whose life he spared, drove faster. He saw the red pickup coming up on him until the chrome grill filled his mirror. Jerry cherishes the well-worn path from office to bed—a doorway, a staircase, a parking lot, two freeways, a left turn past the taco stand. He will not be swerved or intimidated, and the man he later pardoned passed on the right filled with rage. He was a big, bald, red-faced, rage-filled, fuck of a man, and Jerry didn't like removing the .44 Magnum from his forehead. But he realized the man had a story: wife, kids, Dachshund, etc. He couldn't pull the trigger, even in his imagination. So he pardoned the man and tried to sleep. Accepting, as always, that the world just isn't set up for naps.

Jerry's wife, Elise, comes home each day at five-seventeen, drops her purse by the front door, sorts through the mail and walks heavily up the stairs. Jerry can hear her thighs rub together while he pretends to sleep. He's past seeing her as sexual and assumes the rest of the world feels the same. They stay together out of habit, fear inflation, have twenty years left on their variable rate mortgage, contribute the maximum to their IRAs, remain childless except in their nightmares.

Jerry had not wanted a child. For years Elise had urged him to give her a baby, but he had always resisted. He thought it would make him feel older. He thought it would make too much noise. He thought it would it make him tired. She wore him down, but it was only their inability to conceive that made Jerry really want a child. Each painful step: the tests, the taking temperatures, the stacked pillows, the boxer shorts made Jerry want one even more. He thought about all the things he would tell a son, all the things he would warn a daughter. When Elise finally conceived, they bought an expensive Italian crib and set it up in their old office and touched it each time they passed. They argued over names and researched homeopathic morning sickness remedies and, in the third trimester, began counting kicks per their OB's instructions. Each night, they had two hours to count twenty kicks, but the baby was active and the procedure often took ten minutes or less. But the kicks stopped. They made a conscious effort not to panic and waited, thinking she was asleep or resting. Elise shifted positions and took a warm bath. Jerry jiggled her stomach and talked softly to the baby. They called the nurse triage number and she told them to wait another hour. Finally, they were told to go to the emergency room. The doctor on duty was sympathetic. "These things happen," he said.

After they buried their baby girl, they sat in the old office in opposite corners and stared at the crib. Jerry couldn't help but think what a great crib it was. How they had researched it so thoroughly, how there were no government recalls against it and absolutely no chance it could cause any harm to their baby. Elise turned to Jerry and said, "I'm sorry."

And Jerry turned to Elise and said, "It's okay, we can return it. I kept the receipts. We can return all of it."

Jerry wakes up at five-thirty, showers, puts on the clothes he laid out the night before and drives his immaculate, red Honda Civic downtown. He works in Provider Relations at one of San Diego's larger HMOs. Jerry is an eleven-year associate, a level twenty-five in the corporate vernacular. Each level indicates a promotion he has received, a ceremony in which he has received it and a ten-dollar a month raise that always shows up one paycheck later than promised. The associates loathe the ceremonies and joke about the meager raises, the idiot vice-presidents, the persistent denials of corporate downsizing. Sometimes the raises are just enough to throw an associate into a higher tax bracket. They joke about that, too. "What are they going to do, promote me?"

Jerry works in an eight by thirteen cubicle he can decorate however he pleases. He has a desk made of pressed wood and gray plastic veneer, a brand new PC with the best software and a phone with all the pre-programmed speed-dial buttons neatly labeled in blue cursive. If he stands up, he can look out the window and see palm trees in the distance.

Tacked to the beige fabric wall in Jerry's cubicle, surrounded by urgent memos, is a Bert Blyleven baseball card. In '77 Jerry saw Blyleven pitch eight innings of a perfect game. He was disappointed when it was broken up in the ninth, but couldn't forget twenty thousand people giving the pitcher a standing ovation after each out. He became possessed by the desire to pitch and spent long, fleeting afternoons throwing fastballs at a rusty, dirt-filled Hills Brothers can. It made a great sound when he hit it just right, a dull thud as opposed to the high chips from the glancing blows. He lived for that sound but never heard it enough. Much as he tried. After he got bombed in what would be his last minor league game, Jerry's father joked to him about that game in '77. He said Jerry would have been better off seeing a grand slam.

Anna works in the adjacent cubicle. She is tall and thin, has dark roots and wears too much perfume. She is ten years younger than Jerry, thinks he's sweet, always asks him for advice about men and hopes he'll get the hint. Anna's a close-talker and likes the way Jerry loses concentration, the way he can't complete sentences when she's standing next to him. She loves his hands, the gentle way he holds things—like a pen or a clipboard or a Palm Pilot. He holds them like Robins' eggs. She wishes he would hold her like that.

Everyone likes Jerry. He is the ace of Provider Relations, and in a world of faint praise he gets the highest accolade: "You get it, Jerry. You really get it." He gets that his job is saying no to doctors. They ask for things, the doctors. They ask for redundant tests and unnecessary procedures. They practice defensive medicine, perhaps from lawsuit paranoia or perhaps they get a cut from the lab doing the tests. Jerry knows hundreds of ways to say no. Sometimes he sweet-talks them into accepting the limitations. Sometimes he quotes the manual, purposely mispronouncing some of the medical terms for effect. Jerry is usually pleasant, but he can't stand being talked down to and responds by playing dumb.

"I'm sorry sir, could you repeat the question?"

Sometimes he calls them mister instead of doctor and likes the way that pisses them off.

Anna loves to watch him work. Sometimes she'll drift into his cubicle and place a hand on the back of his chair and a hand on the desk by the keyboard. "Put him on hold," she says. "What does he want?"

Jerry tells her he wants a bone marrow transplant, when the rules require a less expensive procedure, or an experimental stent or to routinely test for yeast infections.

"We should let him test for those," she says.

"It's not in the book."

"We wouldn't want someone to come up with a mouthful of cottage cheese."

Jerry turns red and laughs to hide his embarrassment. Anna always asks him to join the group for happy hour. Jerry always says no.

Jerry's last promotion comes in the middle of winter. Elise isn't feeling well and stays in bed. Jerry gets her some tea and dry toast and asks if he can pick up some medicine for her before work. She says no. He figures she is really okay and just wants to play hooky from work, as she often does. He would join her if not for the promotion. It is Friday.

At work, a steady stream of well-wishers make the brief pilgrimage to Jerry's cubicle and extend their congratulations, their condolences, their envy, their relief. Jerry wishes he had room for a second chair, so they could relax and perhaps talk a minute. Mostly, the associates prop both hands against the edges of the cubicle and lean in. "Nice job," they say, or "save some for me." Someone has put a Xeroxed tax table on his desk as a joke. Anna suggests he join the group for happy hour. Jerry says yes.

At one o'clock, the associates from Provider Relations gather, without being told, in the far corner of the cafeteria. They fall into their normal small groups, talk about the upcoming weekend, neglect to make eye contact. McCullough, the new director of Provider Relations, is late. McCullough is young, tan, athletic, like someone Jerry once saw in a mirror. He arrives in a hurry, exudes confidence, shuffles his papers before speaking.

Jerry is one of eight to be honored. He watches uneasily as the other recipients proudly display their red certificates of achievement. He wishes he could share their enthusiasm like he used to. The associates yell and whoop and throw the confetti they've salvaged from the shredding room floor. Jerry has achieved the highest level and comes last.

"Jerry Johnson," says McCullough. There is silence, a brief twitter, the sound of paper dropping to the floor.

"Johnson?"

Jerry slowly walks forward and only briefly catches the anger on Anna's face.

"Johansen, sir."

McCullough glances at the certificate before regaining his smile. "Johansen? The pitcher?"

"I'm sorry, sir?"

"The pitcher. So you're the guy who kills them at softball. Jerry, they speak of you with awe in Customer Service. You used to be pro, right?"

"Double A."

"Oh man, what I wouldn't give. I'll have HR print you a new one of these on Monday. But congratulations. Good work." McCullough uses both hands to shake Jerry's before turning back to the group. "Just one more item. The board has authorized me to let you know that we project steady profits for the next fiscal year and do not anticipate any reductions in force for the foreseeable future. I know many of you have been concerned. We just wanted to set your minds at ease."

Jerry feels more than hears this last speech. He can sense McCullough's booming voice bounce off his back as he returns to his place next to Anna, the only one still watching him. His feet are heavier than he remembers.

"Are you okay?" Anna puts her hand on the small of his back.

"I'm moving up."

"You should complain."

Jerry shrugs.

"Let's go get that cocktail," she says.

For a moment, the thought appeals to Jerry. He thinks about the vodka, the camaraderie, about Anna kissing him full on the lips and pressing her pelvis tightly against his. She might take him home, undress him, make love to him by candlelight. He hopes he can please her, he's so out of practice. She probably won't broach it, he'll have to steer her there. Jerry tries to remember how it goes. He'll have to flirt, find some pretense to get her alone. It'll be awkward. He might be reading her wrong. She won't want her co-workers to see them leave together. They'll take separate cars. She won't want to jump right into bed, he'll have to coax her. It'll be late, Elise will wonder. They'll have to come to work on Monday. What if she doesn't like it? What if he's horrible? What if she just wants to be friends?

"Anna, I don't think I can make it, tonight."

"Oh," she says. Her face shows concern rather than disappointment.

Jerry thinks of Elise, a mug in one hand, a piece of toast in the other. "I think I'm coming down with something."

"Johnson disease?"

Jerry laughs. "Yes, something like that." He feels a dull ache in the back of his head and hears the ocean as Anna hugs him. She tells him to call her if he needs anything. He agrees. He likes the feel of her body against his. Her hair has a taste he can't identify.

Jerry stands for a long time next to his car, fumbling with his keys, trying to remember what he's doing, why he's there. He feels so tired. The air is cold, and he left his jacket in the office. He can see his breath, such a novelty for San Diego. He stops briefly to watch a police helicopter pass. For a moment, Anna reenters his head, and then, yes, he's going home. That's it. Bed. He carefully removes the neon green Club Elise had given him for his thirty-fifth birthday, a record year for car thefts, and tosses it into the passenger seat. The Civic starts the first time.

Traffic is heavier than Jerry anticipated, and he becomes angry when he realizes the backup is being caused by an empty police car on the shoulder. No accident, no traffic stop, nothing. He takes the next exit, Sycamore, a shortcut, finds the left lane and coasts down the long hill towards the light, the Chevron and the Denny's. Two men are mowing grass on the wide median. The right lane is backed up but the left is clear, and Jerry feels powerful, whizzing by the stopped cars on his right. Near the bottom of the hill, just past the footbridge, a forest green Range Rover nudges slowly into the left lane. Jerry sees it. "Don't be an asshole," he says aloud. The Range Rover pauses, Jerry is completely focused on it, willing it to be still, noting all the details he will remember later: the dog barrier between the rear compartment and the back seat, a broken side mirror, an AMA decal, a car seat. And, at the last moment, the man with one eyebrow behind the wheel.

The impact knocks Jerry's Civic into and then over the left curb. He is conscious of an abrasion on his shoulder where the seat belt held him. He feels dazed. Part of the Club has bounced into his lap, and he absent-mindedly grabs it as he detaches the belt and steps onto the grass median.

The Range Rover pulls up behind him, and the man slams the door angrily before checking the damage. He is big and paunchy, wears thick glasses and spasmodically clenches his fists. Jerry stands next to his car and watches. The grass is wet. He wonders if the sprinklers have been on. The man looks at him, and Jerry can't help but focus on the monobrow. He wants to laugh. The man moves forward in a rush. "What the fuck are you doing?"

Jerry throws his arms forward instinctively, forgetting what he carries. The Club bounces off the man's forehead with a tinny ring and a meager thud as it hits the grass. Jerry picks it up. Small pieces of cut grass adhere to the rubber coating. He finds the handle, swings again. The man's forearm is raised but that's not hard to avoid. Jerry likes the sound he makes on contact. His arms vibrate from the stroke. He readjusts his stance, swings again, counts the strokes, lifts his left leg on the downswing. He strikes a fourth time. A fifth time. A sixth time. He loves the sound he's making and wants more. Leather and tin and dirt. Perfection. His mind begins to wander. He wonders if the man has good insurance. Seven. His palms are sweating, and he wishes he had some chalk. Eight. He becomes aware of all the noises and looks up. Cars are slowing on either side of the median, and people have stopped on the footbridge, clutching the chain link canopy to get a better view. They are yelling, car horns are sounding, doors are slamming. The two landscapers are running down the hill. And he realizes he is no longer tired. And he realizes they are cheering for him. Jerry continues for as long as he is able, stopping only briefly between nine and ten to acknowledge the sellout crowd.

Jimmy Jazz

The Bums are at the Beach

Caledonia's legs pump as she races her school chum Katrina Ivankaradzic to the soccer ball on the green at Mission Beach. Another perfect day fades. The coaster rumbles under the high-pitched squeal of a young girl. Time is against us, with the sun perched on the high-dive studying the sea.

—Jimmy. Jimmy, can we steal a moment for adult discussion? She wants to talk about the future, at least the near future, but my mind keeps slipping into the past. I've been here before you see. —Jimmy you have to find a real job, Alaska says.

It's a fair statement, and I mean to consider it judiciously before answering. I've been sitting around the house in my underwear looking for images in the textured plaster walls. Saw plenty of images, but nothing I would call art.

—I'm serious. We have to talk about this. Your unemployment checks are going to run out. I breathe out carefully, to avoid it being construed as a sigh. A bum strikes dirty fingers against the gut strings of a guitar.

—Alaska... I say still unsure how frank I want to speak, yet, careful not to placate.—Alaska... babe... uh... the thing is... I don't want to work.

I rub my hands together even though it isn't cold. Katrina reaches the ball; Caledonia kicks it away, tries to dribble, loses control when her shoelace unfurls, the ball skidders toward the boardwalk, a detour, she circles around... Katrina runs with her arms spread like a gull, mimicking the bird overhead. I wonder why there are no kites in the sky. Caledonia lines up square behind it: kicks! Her right shoe flies turning end over end. The black and white checkered ball rolls on target directly to my feet. —Goal! I yell.

Alaska folds her arms across her chest, shifts the weight from right leg to left. I pick up the ball and give it another sound kick [thud] it soars as with its own wings, bounces then rolls across the grass. They run to fetch it again. Kids are like dogs that way.

—Have you thought about what you want to do? Alaska asks.

—Not really I say. —Don't you think more people should be here playing on the grass?

—Not really, she says.

When I was a kid Mission Beach's Belmont Park was haunted by carnie pitches and the seedy smell of sugar and nicotine. My hippie uncle Eddie and aunty Gretchen brought me weekends. —Every game a winner; a winner in every game. Take a chance and win your gal a prize. A fabulous patina of genuine joy stuck to everything like cotton candy. A dozen sailors mixed with boys and girls in line for caramel apples. Ferris wheel in the sky keep on turning. Fat pigeons choked on popcorn and hot peanuts. The air was filled with risk. The dying amusement park reeked of neglect like a tenement abandoned by an absentee landlord; it was doomed. The asphalt was littered with ticket stubs and smelled faintly of piss. The Wild Angels ruled the wall along the boardwalk; their Harleys lined up in front of Hammel's Surf Shop. Kid comes puking out of The Spinner and heaves soda and hot dog mush at a garbage can, laughing some of it out his nostril. Husky biting flies hung over heaps of rotten garbage. The Funhouse threatened to swallow us whole. But where now the whip-crack of The Wild Mouse and the dizzying heights of The Hammerhead? Carted off, I suspect, to carnivals in Picqua, Ohio and Patchogue, New York. What happened to the rock-n-bobsled that crushed our family together? ¿Donde esta el sideshow? The hideous laughter ricochets through the universe. The crab people live! A skywriting bi-plane scrawls the word COPPERTONE between us and the sun. What about the dime-toss where you could win a KISS, Love Gun mirror, a Hang-Ten-foot ashtray or a troll with yellow hair?

Ring the bell with a hammer! Pop the balloon with a dart! Lasso the milk bottle! Toss a softball into a peach basket! Where we gonna find a goddam milk bottle and/or peach basket when the millennium hits?

The coaster rumbles under the high-pitched squeal of a young girl.

First they outlawed horse diving off the pier; then one night they took the gymnast rings off the beach and the next thing you know the long-chained swings have been replaced by short chains.

My mother used to swim at The Plunge when it was a warm saltwater bathhouse in 52. Flappers held hands here with their misters in 31 doncha know. They tore down the crumbling Spanish plaster building and built a glass and steel greenhouse over the old pool. It's part of a fitness gym now. They took out the high dive and the low dive and put up a sign with rules like NO DIVING and waivers to be signed at the front desk. They bleached the old mildew smell and let the chlorinated fog of the 70's dissipate.

They.

They built a mall around the Giant Dipper roller coaster. Constructed in 25 by a crew of men hired by John D. Spreckels;

and burned down in 76 by arsonists trying to keep warm. Rebuilt by re-development money in 87. They put in a McDonald's to pay the rent. Added a slow-turning baby carousel. The park is very clean now, sterile, and deceptively safe. You can use the restroom now. But that rickety old wooden track will still break your neck and your back. Eeeeeeeeee!

Still, I can't understand why the two million people of this city aren't at the beach to watch the sun set every night.

A tourist tries to snap a photo of the ocean that doesn't have a bum lingering in the background. The coaster rumbles under the high-pitched squeal of a young girl. Two gulls peck a discarded potato, until one flies with it out to sea. A host of sun-blackened winos gambol along the cement wall of the boardwalk drinking beer. A radio plays Zepplin. —And she's buying the stairway...

—If you're not going to get a job, tell me what you think we're supposed to do for money. You know rent? Alaska says. I look at her, shrug my shoulders. I can taste the salt air on my lips.

—I dunno. Things like that take care of themselves. It always works out, I say.

Caledonia jogs up holding the ball, against her tummy.

—Daddy, mommy can we play Monkey in the Middle?

—Sounds like fun, I say. —You're the monkey. She tosses the ball up in the air, takes her place in the middle.

—Caledonia is a monkey, a monkey monkey monkey... I like to tease her saying that we got her from the zoo, shaved her and taught her to speak. She usually plays along acting infuriated. This we call our repartee. I kick the ball to Alaska who kicks it past Caledonia to Katrina trying to keep it away.

We laugh, kick. I can hear the waves breaking on the shore. I kick the ball to Caledonia. —Now I'm the monkey. [Ooo Ooo Ooo.] I make sound effects. I scratch under my armpits and jump up and down. I turn a somersault on the grass.

The girls laugh.

At this point this old orange-skinned rumguzzler leaves his place on the wall and approaches us. He walks without apprehension, like a man driven by an idea. Alaska looks at me like I should do something, or be ready to do something. I expect him to ask for change or a cigarette.

—I used to play soccer when I was a kid in Rhode Island, he says from about two body-lengths away. Alaska looks at him like a mother mountain lion.

—So you came out here from Rhode Island? I ask.

—Ya, among other places. Lived in Hawaii too. I been all over, the rumguzzler says. The girls continue kicking the ball. —My

name's Pete. Pete's wearing faded blue denim jeans and a dirty
button-up shirt. The frayed cuffs on the jeans are wet like he's
been walking the beach with his shoes off. His white tennis shoes
don't fit right, probably a size too big.

—Can I play? he asks. He looks at me. —Don't worry. If you
want me to leave, say the word. He sweeps his hand out to the
horizon. I guess he means he'll vanish, become invisible. Or
return to the sea. Caledonia hops back in the middle. Alaska
kicks the ball to Katrina, but she kicks it off the side of her foot
and it rolls right up to the bum's feet. It's funny how a triangle
becomes a square, doubling its size, by adding one point. —My
name's Pete, he says again. —What's yours? He kicks the ball to
me. Caledonia sidesteps toward it and intercepts.

—I'm Jimmy.

—Caledonia.

—Katrina.

—I'm Marianne, Alaska says proffering a pseudonym. I forget
that you can lie to strangers. You can invent and make up per-
sons and personalities. I wish I'd made up a name too.

I expect Caledonia to say, YOU'RE NOT MARIANNE, but
instead she points at the rumguzzler and says —You're in the
middle.

Pete takes his spot. We kick the ball past him. He moves to
get it, spins, swings a leg up and falls on the grass. He's schnock-
ered. He gets up. Caledonia kicks the ball to Katrina, back to
Alaska, across to Caledonia. Over to me. He can't get the ball. We
have him turning circles, dizzy, so that he falls at more frequent
intervals.

—Okay girls, in soccer you have to use your head, think, he
says tapping a dirty finger on his skull. Caledonia kicks it past
him. Cynical me thinking, Ya, look where it got me, I'm a wino. I
live under the pier at the beach. Then I remember the time Alaska
and I made love under that pier, the moonless night was so dark
we couldn't see each other under there. Eventually Pete gets the
ball. He loses equilibrium as he kicks it, falls again. Katrina's in
the middle. We've extended our family. Uncle Pete smiles reveal-
ing a broken tooth. He has a scab on his forehead. He smells like
stale brew, and something beyond body odor: sweat fermented &
distilled. And kelp. He smells like dead kelp. When he kicks the
ball to Caledonia he does a soft baby kick so dainty like he might
hurt her. She puts a solid leg to it and sends the ball rocketing
past him. He jogs to chase it. I guess bums are like dogs too.

The sun sets, a brilliant explosion of pink over the Pacific.
There's some green in it, you see the blue, some purple. It's time

to go. It's clear that Pete wants to keep playing. —Hey Pete, we have to go now, I say. He steps up close to me like he wants to shake my hand.

—I had a great time, he says. He puts his hand up for a high five. I clap my hand against his. He gets a five from the girls too. Caledonia smacks his hand [slap.] Katrina doesn't want to touch him, but he waits hand vertical until she slaps it. He approaches Marianne for the final five and includes a warm-fuzzy elbow squeeze. —Thanks mama, he says. —Thanks for letting me play. Pete waves. —I love you, he calls. That was never a problem for his generation; it was in every song.

We pile into the car. I see Pete walking over the grassy knoll silhouetted against ocean. He waves again. We all wave back.

—Was that guy poor? Caledonia asks.

—That guy was drunk, I say.

—I smelled alcohol on his breath, Alaska says.

—I smelled drugs on his shoelaces, Katrina says. We return home after renting videos and purchasing a half-gallon of cookies and cream ice cream.

Ella deCastro Baron

weather forecast

Clouds in the morning giving way to perfect sunshine
70s beaches/80s inland

on the answering machine my sister scattered
a pile of glass for me to gulp down
call me as soon as possible
i chewed
i bled
i dialed and spat

it's "invasive lobular carcinoma" i'm not sure what that all
means her left breast mom's overwhelmed that's why i'm calling
behind the nipple the size of a silver dollar i suggested she have
them both removed just in case just in case mammograms only
find half of them we won't know about chemo and radiation
until after they check her nodes can you come up next week
we'll have your birthday here and you can play with the girls
they miss you we didn't expect a visit until april the baby's here
say hi to your auntie she's grumpy i better go put her down for
her nap i'll call you tomorrow

                                                                     pray.

oh and it's the usual unpredictable weather do you have a warm coat
we never know these days see you soon

outside the sun all toasty
with its nose turned sideways
like bliss it smacks me ignorant
snides me saying who cares if it's winter
this is my kind of town
let them wear tank tops and carry sweaters
in their back pockets
those skeptics
still
the daylight's the only thing keeping me
from punching my head
through the coffee table's glare

i climb the stool in the closet
find the wool sweater out of reach
on the top shelf

sun fumes outside my window
tapping like fingers annoyed
unable to reach me
and burn at my pallid face
while the dross of my denial drips
my mouth sputtering red

Photo by Hendrix Knowells

Hoops

Chris Baron

OB Rec

When I was 22, I got addicted. Everyday, I woke up with one thing on my mind: Basketball. It wasn't that I had nothing else to do-after all, I was trying to finish school, working as a bartender, and attempting to maintain a healthy social life—which is probably what brought me to Newport Ave. in the first place. Somewhere along the way, a good friend called me up one morning and said, "Hey, it's raining. Let's skip surfing and play hoops down at the OB Rec."

After that morning, my buddy Mike and I spent almost every day at the Ocean Beach Recreation Center: a small box of hardwood with two shortened basketball courts. In the mornings, there were luncheons for senior citizens, but by 11:59, basketballs were bouncing while the card tables were folding away, and by 12:03, people were shooting for teams. It's all we wanted to do, but why? There was no prize, no money in it; it was a beautiful day outside, but we chose to run back and forth, swearing at each other in a dark and sweaty gym. It might have been addiction, but it was also community.

Human beings live in communities. There is no escaping it. Sometimes we like to imagine that we are soloists, but we are all a part of the band in one way or another. All over San Diego, there are communities of people who live together, hang out together, and watch out for each other. Community is what makes life on this planet bearable. As a kid growing up in New York City, I remember riding the subway out to Brooklyn to visit my grandparents. I was mystified by the community of old Jewish men playing cards on the stoops of the houses while their wives kvetched and gossiped about who was coming and going on that sun-baked street. Even though it freaked me out, it was still a community. It was the only place where bingo winnings, grandchildren, and an endless list of ailments, surgeries, and bodily functions could be talked about without judgment.

We need the space and comfort of these places and people to stretch out and be who we are, who we want to be. If you drive down to Tourmaline beach, you will find "it" as a group of surfers drinking, laughing and blasting "Rambling Man" from an old camper. In South Mission, you can stop by the Pennant and see the same folks talking about the same thing under the same sun. But have you ever wondered what makes any one of these communities unique? Common unity. If we are alone, we see ourselves as too weak, too strong, or even too alone. We need the common unity to breathe truth into us, and to make us who we are.

When I first went to the Rec, nothing else mattered except playing hoops. I was late to work, I skipped class, had girlfriends leave me, jobs fire me, twisted my ankles, broke a finger, had stitches in my eye and in my chin, punched and been punched, yelled and was yelled at, said things I thought I wasn't capable of saying, been called "slacker," "white boy," "no good," "slow motherfucker," "worthless," and "fool." Why would someone go through this?

It's just a game, isn't it?

The answer is in those other moments where you are called "unstoppable," when every shot is falling perfectly through the net strings, your body is fit, your mind indomitable, when you become the "go to" guy on your team. It's when you hit the game winner against a trash talker and lift your fist and scream, when your teammate slaps your shoulder and nods, "good pass," and you find yourself inexorably bound to a team of other guys who you may or may not have known before the game started. You trust them, push them, hope for them, set them up to succeed, and get their back no matter what, and when the air is so thick in the gym that it's hard to breathe, there is that chance, without any excuses, to push ourselves to our limits.

They were all there, brand new Air Jordan's right next to old school Converse All-Stars: alcoholics, ex-high school stars, hippies, dreadlocks, guys who were so stoned they could barely open their eyes to see the ball, surfers marooned without waves, retired college players, landscapers who wrap it up early, teachers off for the summer. Soon enough, we found ourselves a part of this crazy community. We never knew that there was actually a community of people who spent their days at the Rec, going at it to "fifteen-by-two" every single day like a church of the faithful, desperate to express themselves, longing to be accepted, and to just play ball.

Ten years later, after moving around, playing at other Recs, working my career, moving on to occasional Wednesday night leagues and Sunday morning games with friends, I found myself back at the Ocean Beach Recreation Center, and immediately, before my eyes had even adjusted to the dimness of the sweatbox, I heard Pat's crumbled voice, "Yo Chris, we need one, wanna run next over here?" "Sure." I replied, and it was on.

It was as if I had never left. They were all still here: Pat, the landscaper who shoots from the side of his head but makes it every time. Jon, the sun-pocked, rock of a man who played at the Rec since just after it opened over fifty years ago. Sean, who shoots nothing but hook shots, even if he is under the rim (and always seems to make it). Even the young kids, who just a few years ago would run around underneath our feet trying to sneak in shots between games, had all grown up and now played at Point Loma High School. Some had even moved on to play college ball. All of these guys, these coaching nightmares and basketball rebels had become symbols of consistency, strength, and home. They remain, no matter what—September 11, war in Iraq, inflation, deflation, even Starbucks in OB. These guys are here, and here for each other.

That day, I saw Richard's familiar dreads bouncing around the court. Even though the only times I had ever hung out with him were at the Rec, I knew enough to care that he had gone from working odd jobs to owning his own business and raising a new daughter. He looked up at me when I asked him why we spend our days here, and he smiled and said confidently, "Where else can you go in this world where being different isn't an issue?"

I did run next, and we won. I got four games in that day. Still playing to fifteen-by-two.

There are young, familiar faces now starting to carve out their careers. McCall, a sophomore at Point Loma High School, was just a little punk last time I saw him, one of the kids who always tried to play with the big guys. Now he is a force. He'll drive every time if you don't hold him outside, and if you let him breathe, he'll drop a jumper on your head.

I remember feeling like that. Like all that mattered was playing. I wanted to dominate, I wanted to take all the shots, make the cleanest passes, get the breakaway and almost dunk. Sure, there were days when I said to myself, "Couldn't I be putting time into more meaningful adventures? I mean, after all, it's not like I am ever going to do anything with basketball." So far the highlight of my career was placing second at the Bill Walton three-on-three tournament.

But I'm not like that anymore. Now, I want to get a good sweat; I want to check in and see how people are doing. I want to get a few good games in, try and compete. It's more challenging now as seasons change in my life, and my drive to dominate has been replaced by my desire to be simply competitive. So standing there at the OB Rec the other day, I turned to Jeff, a high-flying athlete, always in a backwards hat, "This is the worst slump of my life," I muttered. He smiled; he knew what I was talking about. I found myself in the worst slump of my "basketball career," but we all go through this, and yet, we still want to be here. In these moments, it isn't about hoops, it's about community, because even though we are playing basketball, over in the community room, kids are doing arts and crafts, adults are taking yoga class-es, and people from the neighborhood are holding meetings. Parents can get free childcare, and there are always activities happening on the weekends.

I asked Peter, who works at the Rec Center, why he thought people come to the Rec so regularly and for so many years. "They come to argue," he said. I laughed, but I don't think he was jok-ing. "Most like to argue, that's why they come here: to relieve stress, play ball and yell at each other."

It's true though, people do argue, sometimes ferociously. After all, there are no referees, and it is left up to the individual to call their own fouls and honorably carry out the "rules" of basketball.

One guy who has seen a lot of arguments at the Rec is Terry. He has been coming here for almost 25 years. He wears yellow and blue dishwashing gloves so that he can get a better grip on the ball. He says that if everyone just tried it, we would never go back. Most people couldn't pull this off, but somehow, at the OB Rec, it just seems to fit. He was an elementary school all-star, who started his career shooting a ball through a wooden circle nailed to a tree. He comes for exercise, and for fun and competition, but he also comes for community. I think it is possible that all of these ingredients blend together to keep him seeming so young. Terry is 50, but you wouldn't know it by watching him play basketball. "It keeps me young," he says. "You don't see many places where guys over 50 play basketball everyday." About all the arguing on the court he says, "Yeah man, we argue, but at the end of the day, man, we are back hanging at my house, drinking a few pops."

In the meantime, there is an unspoken code on the basket-ball court. The Rec is full of guys who play at different levels, and there is a game here for everyone. Rich, nicknamed "Filthy," plays at a higher level than most at the Rec—he played college ball and currently plays for the Rocky Point Tiburones, a semi-pro basket-ball team in Mexico. Rich plays ball for a living. For most, this is just a far-flung dream, but Rich comes to The Rec in the off-sea-son to work on his game. He likes The Rec because of the laid-back OB society where "you know everybody." Rich is laid back himself, a regular, and one of the faces you are glad to see when you walk in the gym. No one knows more about the unspoken code of pickup basketball than Rich. Many may look up to him as some kind of leader in this community, but Rich admits that he might not be the best one to lead.

When I asked Rich if he felt like he was a role model at The Rec, he smiled earnestly, "I lead by example, but all my examples are not good." Instead, Rich is an enforcer. I have seen guys come in the gym for the first time, hit some good shots, and start to trash talk one of the other regulars, maybe throw out a comment like, "C'mon old man," or just give a cocky look. Rich doesn't stand for that, and I have seen days where guys have walked out in the middle of the game with Rich close behind, barking at them.

"I give 10 times what I get," Rich tells me. "With my lack of size, I make up for it with aggression and trash talk. If I have to feel the pain physically, then I want them to feel it mentally." So while Rich was learning to take elbows to the body, he learned to "elbow them in their mind."

He continues, looking around as the yoga crowd starts to wander in.

"It's about basketball etiquette and integrity. You have to expect a sportsman's etiquette when you come into a gym with regulars, give them respect. So if they don't give respect, I just give back 10 times the trash talk that's being given to someone else."

Unfortunately, sometimes some of those "not so good" examples leak out and aggression takes over, but he is the first to admit that. "People mean more than the game itself, and I have respect for these regulars that come here."

One of the Yoga ladies pets Rich's mean-looking, pit bull-like dog, silhouetted in the doorway. It drools and wags its tail at the lady.

"You can pet him!" Rich calls out, "He's a family dog. He's all about the love."

He turns back to me, "OB Rec is a great place to play," he says, "because you have a better mixture of age, race, and temperaments."

Somehow, the people who come to The Rec cross over socioeconomic, racial, and age boundaries and form connections that diversity trainers are paid thousands of dollars to teach about in corporate America.

With so many groups, organizations, causes and ideologies artificially calling us to come together and share our lives, we ought to be grateful when we find ourselves as part of a truth, a common unity, a place of authenticity and trust. We should care for it and be sure that all are invited to be a part as long as they bring their real selves. This is how it is at The Rec Community.

At the end of each conversation, whether it was Joe, the Point Loma Varsity basketball Coach who coaches everyone through his skill and encouragement, Mike, Pat, or Chris, who consistently greet everyone with a smile and a competitive game, or whether it is the "real" old guys who play in the leagues here every week, meeting at 5am Sunday morning like they have through the decades, all of them assured me that they would always squeeze in time for basketball.

All hope to remain regulars at the OB Rec, that even after their fires have faded, they would be here, talking trash, screaming at each other, elbowing each other, holding each other up, helping one another to forget the pain of the day, the stress of the outside world, the frustrations of relationships and the strained expectations of unfulfilled dreams.

I know now how fortunate I am to count myself as one of them. For me, at The Rec, community is central, morality is easy and natural, respect is a gift, and hope is awake and vibrant, always waiting in every move, every fade-away jump shot, every lay-up, every rebound, and every perfect dish. In every game, there is a chance to become more than who we are.

Scott Tinley

Eros, Poseidon and Me
"Darkness, darkness, be my pillow..."
Jesse Colin Young, singer, songwriter

There was no place to go. No one to call, if only just to file the edge off or sharpen it so that it might open a bottle, open a book, say a prayer, say goddamn.

I looked at my dog. He knew. Animals are smarter than men. On the surface, they look like animals. Cut them open and you won't find bones and meat, just one big heart taking up their entire insides.

Buddy dog-stepped across the room, looked at me with real dog eyes, the kind of knowing, "been-there-it-hurts-like-a-motherfucker-don't-it?" eyes. But he didn't try and lick me or curl up at my feet, just let me fall through the hole in myself to land on some canopy of malignant influence. On the surface things are always deceiving. But dogs have a different kind of depth perception.

The little guy just stared, like he was trying to soak some of the pain right out of me, absorb it into his own hardened dog-heart. Maybe he knew the landscape behind me was burning and my only escape was the Great Blue Firebreak.

A precise emotion seeks a precise expression. There were only two options left and I knew she would be pissed if the blood stained the new beige carpet. I felt an honest conspiracy move in under the fog of self-deceit, blowing it away like smoke rings in the wind. It was a cold proposition, unnamable, immutable.

How hard can it be to snatch something real from the ever-fleeting? To do a thing for the thing's sake? To see the rottenness in life but deny the smell and reach for the broom?

But how fortunate was I to have my own version of a Betty Ford Center two blocks away? And it covers three-fourths of the planet.

I put an old 3/2 mm wetsuit in my backpack, tossed some wax, the rest of some half-empty bottle of wine and a mushy apple in the front basket. I grabbed the first board out of the rack and tucked it under my arm.

I don't remember coasting down the hill on my bike or scrambling down the bluff as the sun left its mark on the hellish day. I couldn't tell you if it was a beautiful sunset or a cloudy dusk. All I knew is that it was getting dark all the way around, the sea and the sky welding at the horizon.

Buddy stood on the shore and pointed like a bird dog. Strange for a mutt. Go home Buddy. Oh forget it. Suit yourself. I took a bite of the apple and tossed the core into the sand watching little grains stick to it like memory to the soft part of the brain.

I really thought I knew her. When it came to stature, she put the rest of us downstream. It wasn't like I'd been living with a person, more like I'd been living with my imagination of her potential. The silence between us was growing louder every day.

Paddling out I began to notice things I hadn't before: the way the cold water seeps in around your knees before your waist, the way the little wake comes off the tip of your board in angular vees, going somewhere, no where. I noticed how the shallow spots on the reef created circular boils on the fast-dropping tide, pulling water, energy and life from its center back into some black hole beneath the surface, a place from which that life and water were born.

There was only one other guy out, one other surfer in the lightest part of the dark hoping maybe, for one last toothy wave of a two-hour session. He only needed a ride in, didn't have to worry about being caught from behind.

I paddled right by him, avoiding his stare. Nothing he could say would've made a difference. He was nothing.

No, that's not what I meant to say. He was another human being and I didn't know anything about him. Maybe he just got out of the joint and hadn't surfed for three years. Maybe he was a "trustafarian" who surfed every day to avoid the boredom of excess. I turned my head just enough and lifted my chin in some prison greeting then tried not to crawl back inside myself, tried to create symbols out of natural elements.

"Word," I said.

"Word up," he replied.

He paddled away. I hadn't erased him but I hadn't really created him either. I didn't see him leave the water or walk up the path, only heard a single dog bark, once.

When I looked straight west again, the day had taken its chasms with it but left its cliffs. Fair enough. Out of the corner a big set started to well up on the outside reef. How far had this wave traveled only to finally release its energy here in 6 feet of black, kelpy salt water? And then lie down and die.

I paddled hard, spun at the last minute and dropped in, one with the falling lip, Rosetta Stone in sync. At the bottom, I laid it over hard and felt the board bite deep into the face, anger and tension in some primal battle with regret and despair. My wake gouged at the beauty, then filled in with guilt.

What did the poet say?

"The longer we were together, the closer we grew apart." I could've done better with her.

The wave in front now, feeling the rocky bottom, standing up, begging to envelop, some child bringing home a picture made at school.

"Look, Dad. Look at this picture I made for you!"

Look, son, look at this wave I made for you.

Inside now, an absence of feeling in my heart, there's darkness at the wave's circular core. But it is a place of hope and I strain towards a faint pulsing glow, the glimmer of some left over refracted light off the bluff as I squirt out onto a broad, nurturing shoulder.

What did the German Jew, the one searching for meaning say when he was released?

"What is to give light must endure burning."

I used to recite those kinds of things, and she'd laugh, say, "That's cute, honey."

Paddling back out, I glanced over at a sea lion. He held my stare and returned an odd, queer look, as if to say, "I can do that." The ocean could swallow him up and get nothing on him. He'd make an obscenely joyous sound. You'd remember him. The moment would empower you.

The opaque roof above me had hemorrhaged all reflection by then and I surfed by feel, wondering what it would be like to get in a fight with a shark right there, then. I don't fear them. It's more dangerous to live in the land of humans walking around, terra firma erect, dangerous and disloyal.

And I thought, what an interesting way to die, to lose a fight with an animal that is made to kill, as listed on page twenty-four in the next day's obits.

"A killing machine," they would say, "that came out from beneath the ocean's surface to rip the man's leg off." The autopsy would say that, "he had an enlarged heart." It wouldn't say that it was broken.

It would be a fitting death. Still, I would fight like hell. Same as if a stranger came into my house and I was born hungry.

Some hint of moon must've watched this cathartic play. The world was breathing, shrinking and expanding. I used to lie next to her at night and wonder why God had given me such a creature.

And now, sometime after midnight that great block of ice that had settled in my chest began to melt. I wanted to believe that shit about truth at first light but I felt that it was the night, the absence of external fire, the melding of one day into the next, that opens the gates.

And I was bleeding now out every pore. It was something, a thing beyond the sad wisdom of compromise. Then the rain started; a loud rain, hard in noise but soft on the back of my neck.

I am living outside of man's law of common sense, engaged in the Laws of Nature. In the beginning she was close to a real thing. Now, it seems, she needs something artificial to set off the authentic. She used to change her eye colors with glass lenses. Other times her eyes would look dead, like she had lost them somewhere and then had found them at a half-yearly sale.

I am right there, making my own truth, rehearsing my own death.

I am alive.

Almost imperceptible at first, I begin to notice it first in the waves I choose and the way I surf them. Then in my relationship with the ocean surface, the way my board sits gently upon this sheet of smooth black ice, the way my hands softly make quiet little circles on its skin. And then with my self, the way I feel towards my rightful place among these elements.

I cannot see the advancing swell but I sense something gathering up, waiting for me, if I have the courage. I paddle hard for the horizon, the lower stars blocked by this advancing swell. Harder now, pulling at still water, onward to meet a new Her.

She can't be changed, nor could I willfully submit. This is *Her* home. I am a guest. But I am open to invitation and experience, each pore on my skin a swimming pool, water spinning down as whirling thoughts. I used to think of a wave as a plate glass window waiting for a brick. But now I have to climb upon Her back and unsheathe guilty arrows with each slice of my fin and movement of my board. I lay them down and step on their past.

When it finally comes, it is like no wave I have ever ridden: big but not unwieldy, imperfect in shape and texture, its symmetry uneven and raw. There is a low growl from a lower storm cloud. Her unmasked sensuality, a single finger asking—come here, an irresistible indulgence without relevance to time or space. The night is fresh.

And she carries me like no other wave has. I feel as if I should be taking an oath or something; that I cannot even stand to ride but only lay down, prostrate, my face close to Hers. Our breasts a puzzle in sync, my skin wanted to meld with her surface but shielded by a glass vehicle, my fear coming right up against the nature of things. She is electric.

Following the shelf, I ride until my fins hit the sandy shore and I stay there, motionless, textured, breathing. A moon bends under a passing cloud. A phosphorescent edge of foam is switched on. My lips turn crescent.

I let the match burn through to the end and stood up, grabbed my board and walked toward the cliff. My footsteps kicked sand into the air. The tide has its way.

She is gone. They are gone. Buddy and I are right here, our eyes seeking purchase in simple human animalness, watching our breath go up and out.

And in that presence, a strange confluence spun me and I saw the old her in the unfolding, stumbling in the dark, digging in bent trash cans outside the theater looking for someone new to play her part. We are making choices in the moment; choices that matter, that hurt. They overlap like a Venn diagram filling an ambiguous vacuum, no longer linear, no longer anything worthy of love as a label. It's more like libel. And all that wonderfully edible mayhem in her, dying and living not in the sunrise but in every south wind, angry at the high noon moon; she paints skies in colors that fight each other on the pallet. I thank her for that and say goodbye to her gentle violence and half-dead eyes.

I've met someone else, I say to myself, tasting the words. She comes and goes. We are...old friends.

Walking back up the wet clay trail, Buddy waits for me at the top, laughing, I imagine, at how humans confuse absolution and the absolute. I know that surfing and what is left of my life are there now glaring back in the headlights of a passing train, straining to deny reality and then defining something real in the long broken line of possibilities.

I am not haunted by Her.

Sandra Alcosser

Throughout the Duration of a Pulse the Heart Changes Form

                    Tonight as you return
                to our blue sea cottage, see
            how the rosewood horse gleams.
I have touched everything.
The white hibiscus
        hover against the window,
                their red stamens craned like candlewicks.
                    Winter in this rain-soaked village,
                    still, the fleshy roses bloom, evenings
                sweeten with the smoke of eucalyptus.
        I put out a bowl of pecans. I sweep
the white tile floor one, two, three times.
 How nervous your absence
        makes our friends, as if by marriage
            we were blown into a single figurine.
                    After many weeks alone, we will
                    turn our simple lives toward
                each other. I bathe my limbs carefully.
        I perfume the blood beats.
As the yellow spider crawls
into the mouth of the yellow lily
        or the butterfly brushes against the blanketflower's eye—
            drinks there—so too I've flourished
                with each stroke of the body.
                    Though nights when I could not find
                a decent voice on the radio, outside my window
    starlings filled the pomegranates, starlings filled the figs.
They ripped open everything. They spit out the seeds.

Heather Eudy

Division of Meat
an Inuit stonecut

This sketch. Two inky balls for hands. Two fists
clenched. But even in the restriction of blood flow oxygen
        pulsates for an opening closer to air, closer
to the past-membrane wishing it had found another matter
        to rest within. Hands are drums.   The music
they make   caterpillar fingers   oak leaf veins
        or is that because we are from the West the only way
we traveled here was   via the uterus
        landed plump on the rock of a San Diego hospital bed.

Thank the viewer for her time though she failed to mention
        the triangles endlessly tracing   the torso attempting
to fit isosceles into sphere. Only parts of us can be
        measured the rest we don't want to define
though
        I attempt libation
until no skin
        is dry but the first portion touched
so I try again this time faster
        each cell
I want to fulfill simultaneously
        but in this frame
I am incapable.
        I become all tongue all salt and water
my lovers have never known
        such
                pleasure. That is what rivers give to the oceans
as they enter the blur between two bodies.

But the feet. What about the feet? Two clumsy sticks
balancing geometry against gravity.
        How can the anteriors of our vertebrate bodies sit
upright in waking
when the cats lie down after meals and our mouths are arrows
        for a compass like the brain of a frog?
To sustain equilibrium she must rotate infinitely.
        She'll spin like that on your skull.
You start believing she's dancing. Though bone and ribbed
skin
        feel like a barrier, mouths circle space.
Look at that head. One horizontal clump of hair
        is the only thing
to stop it.

Steve Kowit

To Tell the Literal Truth

is the trick by which poetry, Rico was saying, anchors itself
to the actual world (I had been rash enough to suggest
that in art the literal truth doesn't matter a bit),
when a coiled rattler, a good four feet of her, stretched
in the heat on the ill-marked Moorfred Rivercrest trail
we'd been hiking, startled us out of our chatter.
We didn't breathe, gave her a wide berth, & were safely past,
when Zoly, our Aussie companion, who'd just gotten back
from a month-long dig in the outback pits of Rodinga
—Zoly, who cares not a whit for epistemological theory—
did something I'll never forget: in one swift motion swiveled,
bent & grabbed for her throat, the other hand closing
above that whiplash of rattles, then, with a grin, rose to his feet.
The creature writhed in his hands, buzzed with her hideous
rattlers, while she hissed with her godawful tongues
& tried to break free. Rico & me, we jumped back in terror.
Zoly, holding her out for us to admire, said "Crotalus atrox:
Western Diamondback. Marvelous specimen, no?"
I could care less what it was called. I took another step back.
Zoly strode to an outcrop of boulders a few yards away,
& gently as setting a kid in its crib, & with only the tiniest
flourish—the sort a jaunty conductor or close-up
magician might make— tossed the thing free.
It vanished, instantaneously, slithering into the rocks.
I took a deep breath & relaxed. From where we stood,
on that rise, you could make out the Salton Sea, far
to the east, & the undulant floor of the desert a long drop below,
endless & dreamlike. "Amazing!" Rico mumbled
under his breath, lifting his Padres cap & rubbing the sweat
from his brow. But whether he meant the vista, or snake,
or how quickly it vanished, or what Zoly had done,
or the whole delectable drift of the thing, god only knows.
Listen: In art, the truth—in that sense—doesn't matter.
I made the whole story up. The Aussie. The outback.
The snake. Even the name of the trail. All but the part
where two friends & I argue over the poet's relationship
to the literal fact. Everything else in this poem is a lie.

Estela Eaton

San Diego Girls

For Cassandra

The tenants climb the sherbet steps to flood
the crackling roof. Their tangled echoes lunge
at tracks of planes in waves of blue and blood,
like whales that streak the coast with high-pitched lungs.

The tenants yawn and clutch at weightless hearts:
a massive braid of smoke that cannot hold
the men residing on the ground, who cart
around the sleeping skins of women, old

with longing. They were crowded in the husks
from month to month, until the tenant hosts
agreed to join the other girls who dared

to lose themselves in watercolor dusks
—receding pyramids of faith and lust—
that coo the desert: *Sift us, dust and hair.*

Photo by Jennifer Cost

Kiss My Axle

Lance Newman

Anza Borrego

Walking in, the new pack bites my shoulders.
I can't find my balance in the talus.
Brittle bush. Bajada. Creosote. Sand.
A fly lights in the sweat on my forehead.
Teddy-bear cholla, Mojave hedgehog—
there must be a poem in these words.
In the canyon bottom, five black-throated
sparrows whistle in the smoke trees. A lone
phainopepla sings from an allthorn's top.
How do all these pieces fit together?
Half-dead chamisa drills roots in weathered
schist. Stag-horn cholla rots upright, leaving
bundles of hollow, perforated stems.
When I get to Hidden Springs, I'll drink deep.
My boots crunch one and two and one and two
across the playa's bright caliche floor.
Chert flakes and fire-cracked rocks in the sand
mean Cahuilla ruins. The springs are close.
The trail is marked with popped balloons, rubber
rotted by sun, tied to brush with ribbons.
The spring is dry. A new steel sign, planted
in brittle bush and sage, reads, Hidden Springs.
Still, a thicket of beavertail cactus—
no spines but purple glochids—grows in dust
drifted in a ruin's low, stone circle.
The creosote bush here wears spiky, round
galls and wind makes the lower branches sweep
curved scars in the arroyo's white, white sand.
A scouting raven spots me and croaks once.
Its mate answers and they settle down to wait.
I swing into my pack and curse my legs
and hunt a place to unshoulder this load.
This high desert valley will cool off fast.
Yucca leaves lay scattered on the gravel,
white as bones. Long stalks, felled by wind across
the trail, look like signs saying, Turn right here.
Where bedrock rises from the valley floor,
an old ocotillo—its base a foot

through—divides all at once into fifty
straight branches next to a salt-and-pepper
granite boulder. A young creosote bush
grows between the split halves of another.
Ocotillo, rocks, and brush—no different
from the others that I passed walking in,
but here they make a place, a place that says, Rest.
I drop the pack and sit and watch the sun
fall behind the granite peaks of Buck Ridge.
I cook my soup and eat and feed the dog.
A luna moth drinks water from my pot.
I make the bed by the ocotillo.
A half moon backlights whorls of dime-sized leaves.
Green pith glints through bark like flesh through a scab.
At dawn, a house finch sings from the branches.
Ice crystals rattle in my water jug.
Two potsherds rest in white sand by my bed—
domestic gray ware with thumb-nail ridges.
What makes this place a place is how these things
fell into place like words in a poem,
inviting me in, like they did the one
who shattered this clay pot, spilling water
or dried corn on the ocotillo's roots.

Katherine Melcher
Day-Glo San Diego

Ahh, beautiful San Diego, day-glo San Diego, with your 76 degree weather and your sunny beaches. Your palm trees, ocean breezes, and sunsets. The land of perpetual sunshine and perpetual tans. Of beautiful weather and beautiful people.

I moved to San Diego two and a half years ago, escaping from Portland and thirty-four days straight of rain, thirty-four days of gray skies and a sun so faint that it might as well have been the moon. I would step out into the day with my bright yellow umbrella, ready to combat the gray. But the winds blew, flipped it inside out and broke it in half. Now hanging from the ceiling in a friend's basement, it became a subterranean sun.

So I figured a technicolor San Diego of perennial blue skies, green palms, and magenta flowers would not be so bad. Plus, I had a job waiting for me with Friday afternoons off. I had visions of spending my long weekends in Mexico, in the mountains, and, of course, taking long walks on the beach as the sun sets.

I enjoyed discovering the neocolonial Prado promenade in Balboa Park, the quirky neon street signs in mid-city neighborhoods, and Egyptian-revival buildings adorned with pharoahs and serpents. They all suggested to me that San Diego does not (or at least used to not) take itself too seriously. Somehow, somewhere it has a capacity to dream. I rented a cute little art deco bungalow that fit my preconceived romantic images of early Southern California. As I walked to my bungalow along a sidewalk lined with banana plants, I dreamt of orange groves, health resorts, people seeking adventure, and the glamour and excitement of early Hollywood. I dreamt of a Southern California before it became synonymous with traffic jams and smog. I loved that my neighborhood gave me three coffee shops, a grocery store, and a bank all within walking distance.

I dove into the California lifestyle, or at least a parody of it. I tried boogie boarding, mountain biking, and brunch in La Jolla. I started seeing a therapist. I started seeing a pedicurist. And a Pilates instructor. I lightened my hair and bought a yoga ball. I became conversant on such topics as housing prices, freeway traffic, and American Idol. I found myself driving the two blocks to the grocery store and bank. I searched for grunions and the green flash.

Then I came home one day to find my darling bungalow painted the bright turquoise of Crest. It clashed with the banana plants, the annoying banana plants that I constantly hit my head

Photo by Jennifer Cost

Hacienda Del Sol

on while walking by. My hair was lighter but my thoughts remained dark. Friday afternoon traffic was so bad, I preferred to stay at home. My new polka dotted bikini stayed in the drawer. As the sun set I would stare at it sinking behind the palm trees behind the toothpaste walls of my compound.

In the late spring, I would wake up to an overcast morning and sigh with relief. Gray skies seemed to demand less than sunshine. In the summer, despite being surrounded with pastels, I wore black halter tops and black sandals. In the fall, I would escape to the mountains for a feel of autumn chill and the smell of decaying leaves. No matter how hard I tried to understand, flip-flops with high heels still left me puzzled.

San Diego wasn't living out its dreams, just its delusions. The year-round tropical paradise disguises a fragile, dry Mediterranean climate. In the middle of a three-year drought, we still have lush green grass, gorgeous swimming pools, and decorative fountains. Women remain young by covering their gray and injecting their wrinkles. The nightly news can find nothing more important for a lead than the latest invention in the plastic surgery world. Our great "public sphere" is a shopping mall, Horton Plaza. People can walk in from the street, but security guards keep the homeless and other undesirables out. Thanks to Sea World, we have fireworks every evening, and by the next morning all the trash and dirt has been swept away.

Why are we so afraid of brown leaves, wrinkles, and poverty that we create this world of delusions? Why do we always prefer to cut and cover?

San Diego artist and architect James Hubbell said, "A plastic flower is not beautiful because it does not die." San Diego at times feels like a plastic flower. All its beauty is shielded behind a denial of death.

But with the fall comes the Dia de los Muertos, forest fires, and flash floods. An environment harsh and capricious, not constant and easy, is our reality. Within the drama, there is passion. And from passion, beauty grows.

And there is beauty in San Diego.

There is beauty in Chicano Park.

There is beauty in the hidden canyons winding through neighborhoods in unexpected ways.

There is beauty in the fall hillsides—in the rust colored dried bouquets of buckwheat and the white gray sage. And in the green oaks, cool breezes, and sounds of quail.

There is beauty in the neighborhoods where family-run nail parlors sit next to barber shops, taco shops, and karate academies. Afro-Carribbean dancing, neon signs, Chinese herbs and seven powers of Africa are all neighbors.

There is beauty in the rusting machinery along the bayfront.

There is beauty in the leaning Victorians, with their colorful, peeling paint, as well as in the graffitti murals of Barrio Logan.

There is beauty in the elderly woman stuck in Mission Valley traffic, releasing dandelion fluff piece by piece out the window of her Corolla.

And there is beauty in the sunset. We seem to only appreciate the day when the sun starts setting. The surfers float over the gentle waves, facing west, watching, waiting, searching for the next good break.

The ride always ends with a fall. But that does not stop them.

Photo by Jennifer Cost

The Last Resort

Ed James

The Jumping-Off Place

Chuck woke up to the sound of a car alarm going off down on the street below his room at the Golden West Hotel. He rolled over on his side and stared at the newspaper he had dropped on the floor before falling asleep. It was folded over to page 14 and the headline, "Government Says National Sacrifice Zones Will Never Be Salvaged." Whatever, Chuck thought. He sat up slowly, groaned, and rubbed his eyes until he saw a strange, checkered pattern of light behind his lids. When he opened them there was the blank white wall and his dirty gray pants were on the back of the chair. A car horn blared outside. Chuck grabbed a cigarette out of the pack on the nightstand and lit it with a cheap purple lighter. He took a drag, blew it out, stood up, pulled on his pants, and grabbed a plain white t-shirt out of the top drawer of the dresser. He left the shade down, walked over to the sink and splashed some water on his rugged, pockmarked face. He stared at some old scars and brushed back his short, spiky white hair with his hands. Old and ugly, he thought.

After wiping his face dry with a musty hand towel, Chuck tossed it on top of the dresser and glanced back in the mirror at the skull and cross bones tattooed on his meaty forearm. He was a big, hulking man, still strong for sixty. Nobody got in his way on the street. Chuck sat back down on the bed and put on his scuffed black leather shoes. He was hungry. He got up and walked out of his room, through the dim hallway to the stairs. As he made his way down, Chuck looked at the people sitting in rockers, watching TV. Nobody he cared about. Some guy was nosing around the lobby like the place was a museum. Stupid asshole, Chuck thought. He felt like walking over and laying him out just for the hell of it. In the old days, he would have. Now, he just muttered to himself and walked by the idiot babbling about Fred Astaire in the chair by the door. "Fuck you and Fred Astaire," he growled at the man.

Chuck walked across the middle of Fourth Avenue towards the Moon Café and a woman in a huge truck honked at him when she had to stop to let him pass. He turned around, flipped her off, and glared at her with notable intensity. She drove around him in a huff. "Bitch," Chuck muttered to himself. In the Moon Café, he sat down next to a guy he used to drink with in the Naha before it closed.

"Hey Arnie," Chuck said as he slapped him on the back.

"How's it hangin'?" Arnie replied.

"All the way down my left pants leg," Chuck said with a laugh. The middle-aged Korean woman behind the counter looked at them coolly and walked over to take their orders—two $1.99 breakfast specials and fifty-cent coffees. She wiped down the counter with a wet dishrag but the grease was so thick it still stuck to Chuck's forearms. "I could write my name in this shit," he grumbled to Arnie. Arnie laughed and nodded.

"You remember Big Jack from the Naha?" Arnie asked.

"Sure," said Chuck.

"He died over in the Maryland last week."

"What of?" asked Chuck.

"Don't know, but I heard it took a couple of days until anybody missed him. He was stiff as a board when they found him. Nobody knew who to call."

"Well, I guess somebody's got to give the firemen a reason to stand around and scratch their asses. You ever see how many guys show up just to drag off a corpse?" Chuck said.

"It's like a goddamned block party," Arnie agreed. The food came. They both ate slowly and silently, nursing the runny eggs and charred bacon, sipping the weak, watery coffee. Chuck glanced out the window at a group of pretty young Italian girls in short skirts. One of them dropped something and bent over to pick it up. Chuck felt the blood flowing down below. "I wouldn't mind that," he said as he nudged Arnie.

"Keep dreamin' you old fuck," Arnie said. They laughed and Arnie put down his fork and wiped his plate clean with a piece of dry toast.

"Maybe I'll just jump off the bridge before they have to carry me out past a crowd of strangers," Arnie said.

"Shut the fuck up," said Chuck, "You'll die wanking off in bed and they'll put a picture of your rigor mortis on the front page." Arnie laughed, said goodbye gruffly, left three dollars on the counter, and walked out the door. Chuck finished his coffee and looked over at the woman behind the counter.

"What do you say?" he offered.

"Nothing to you," she said, smiling with cruel pleasure. Chuck smirked, blew her a mock kiss, left two dollars and fifty cents on the counter, and walked out onto Fourth Avenue. Some teenagers in nice new clothes sitting on the sidewalk outside a fancy restaurant asked him for change.

"You're kidding me, right?" Chuck snarled. He thought back to the days when this whole street was full of strip bars, porn theatres, and nickel and dime places. Today you couldn't get a whore without a credit card and the yellow pages. Once he'd left the

Navy, he'd worked as a bartender, a bouncer, a security guard, a hotel desk clerk, and a cashier at a peep show. Now he was just taking checks and squeezing by. Nobody wanted an ugly decrepit geezer to check IDs at the door. Chuck walked by the Hard Rock Café and spit on the sidewalk in front of the door. He crossed the street and lumbered by the mall. The suits and shoppers were out in full force. The pretty young girls with bags didn't look at him and the suits stepped out of his way. It was all too goddamned clean and shiny. He felt like hitting someone. Chuck crossed Broadway and walked past the doorman outside the U.S. Grant. How could he wear that cute little uniform? Chuck shook his head in disgust, hit Third Avenue, and made his way by an office complex, Second Avenue, another office complex, First Avenue, the Greyhound Bus terminal, a 99 cent store, a cheap deli and mini mart, and a barber shop before he came to the Piccadilly Bar, the last outpost on the last remaining block of the old West Broadway.

"Hey Chuck," the bartender said.

"Hey Larry," Chuck said, "How 'bout a draft?" Larry poured one and Chuck paid just as Scottie strolled in the front door. He was wearing an Airborne hat, dark sunglasses, an Army surplus jacket, and camo pants. He walked up to some kids sitting with backpacks, sipping Cokes. They were probably waiting for a bus. Scottie started telling them tall tales about Vietnam and asked the kids to buy him a beer. They did. Chuck waited until the beer had been paid for and yelled, "The only war Scottie ever fought in was with his ex-wife!"

"Fuck you, Chuck!" Scottie yelled.

"Not for all the tea in China!" Chuck shot back. Scottie rushed over to the bar and knocked over Chuck's beer. Chuck stood up and flattened him with one punch. Scottie stayed on his back, mumbling obscenities.

"Take a walk, Chuck," Larry said firmly.

"No problem, Larry," Chuck agreed. He got up, winked at the kids in the corner, and walked out the door, down towards the harbor past the new courthouse, the YMCA, a huge new office tower. Chuck tried to remember where Cindy's Topless A Go-Go had been. When he had been a bouncer there, the girls danced on a tiny stage behind the bar where Little Gus was serving up drinks in a starched white shirt with a black bow tie. After work, Chuck would go over to Downtown Johnny's diner and order a burger or a grilled cheese sandwich. You could sit there for hours as long as you kept buying coffee. He remembered talking all night there with one of the girls from Cindy's and walking with her out into the dawn with a sense of invincibility. "We'll never die," he'd said to her with mock bravado. She had laughed and kissed him lingeringly, passionately. He couldn't remember what had happened to her, sweet thing, and he wasn't sure where any of the old places had been.

Chuck moved on, past the new tower, over the trolley tracks by Santa Fe Station. Sometimes he liked to buy a cup of coffee there, read the paper, and watch the people come and go. Not today though, he didn't feel like it. Chuck kept walking all the way to the harbor, turned right, and trudged by the tourist ships, Anthony's Fish Grotto, and the Star of India. He ignored all the happy, tan people. There weren't any fishing boats left anymore. He sat down by the water and let the breeze gently blow on his face. The sun was bright and hot and the water was deep, deep blue. Chuck felt he was at the end of the world somehow, out of gas. Sometimes he thought he might want to say something, express something, utter a dying croak. There were no words though. And what did he have to say anyway? Chuck thought about jumping in, sinking down, and never coming back up.

Contributors

Sandra Alcosser founded and directs the Master of Fine Arts Program in Creative Writing at San Diego State University each fall, as well as SDSU's International Writers Summer Program at National University of Ireland, Galway 2004-2005. She is Poet-in-Residence for Poets House, New York, The Wildlife Conservation Society and Central Park Zoo, the poetry editor for *Parabola Magazine*, and The Wildlife Conservation Society's *State of the Wild*. Her most recent book of poetry, *Except by Nature*, selected for the National Poetry Series, received four national awards including the James Laughlin Award from the Academy of American Poets. James Tate chose *A Fish to Feed All Hunger*, her first book of poems, for the Associated Writing Program's Award Series in Poetry. She has received numerous other awards including two National Endowment for the Arts fellowships. Her poems have appeared in *The New York Times, The New Yorker, The Paris Review* and the *Push Cart Prize Anthology*.

Adrian Arancibia is a San Diego writer. He is a founding member of the Taco Shop Poets and the arts collaborative Voz Alta. He was born in Iquique, Chile and continues to publish stories, columns and poetry about life as an immigrant living on the border.

Jimmy Santiago Baca's books include: *The Importance of a Piece of Paper* (Grove/Atlantic) and *Winter Poems Along the Rio Grande* (New Directions), as well as, *A Place to Stand, Healing Earthquakes, C-Train & Thirteen Mexicans, Black Mesa Poems, Martin & Meditations on the South Valley*, and *Immigrants in Our Own Land*.

Chris Baron completed his MFA in Poetry in 1998, and is currently on the executive board for the Border Voices Poetry Project. He also teaches English and Writing at San Diego City College while consulting on writing programs in other schools.

Ella deCastro Baron received her MFA from San Diego State University. She teaches Composition, surfs, prays with/writes about those who are chronically ill, and is trying to get more Filipino-American stories onto bookshelves.

Josh Baxt grew up in Northern Virginia and migrated to San Diego in 1990. He has an MFA in creative writing from San

Diego State University and writes for a local nonprofit. In 2002 his play, *Like a War*, was produced for the Fritz Blitz. Josh's work can be found online and in *City Works* where he was a featured local writer. Josh was formerly the director of the San Diego Writing Center.

Matthew Bokovoy is Co-Editor of the *Journal of San Diego History* and an acquisitions editor at the University of Oklahoma Press. He has taught at the University of Pennsylvania, Temple University, University of Nebraska, Kearney, and Oklahoma State University. He is the author of the forthcoming *The Peers of Their White Conquerors: The San Diego Expositions and the Heritage Crusade in the Southwest, 1880-1940*, (Albuquerque: University of New Mexico Press, 2005). He grew up in Coronado.

Angela Elizabeth Boyce was born in Barstow California. She is a California Arts Fellow who currently resides in San Diego.

Sydney Brown lives/writes in La Mesa and teaches creative writing and composition at Grossmont College. "The Role of the Illegal Immigrant in the Local Economy" works with Robert L. Pincus' "The Invisible Town Square: Artists' Collaborations and Media Dramas in America's Biggest Border Town," from the collection *But is it Art?*

Francisco Bustos lives most of the time in Playas de Tijuana, Mexico, with his daughter Quetzalli and wife Nirvana, and sometimes in Chula Vista CA. He teaches English and Composition at Southwestern College, plays guitar, and writes about border culture.

Marilyn Chin is the author of *Dwarf Bamboo, The Phoenix Gone, The Terrace Empty,* and *Rhapsody in Plain Yellow*. She has won numerous awards for her poetry and is featured in a variety of anthologies, including *The Norton Anthology of Modern and Contemporary Poetry, The Norton Introduction to Poetry, The Oxford Anthology of Modern American Poetry, Unsettling America, The Open Boat,* and *The Best American Poetry of l996*. Born in Hong Kong, Chin lives in San Diego and co-directs the MFA Program at San Diego State University.

Leilani Clark is an educator, writer and musician who lives in the Logan Heights area of San Diego. She self-publishes a bi-yearly 'zine entitled *A Watcher of Birds*.

marion cloete was raised in the vibrant city of Cape Town, South Africa, in the shadows of Table Mountain and Apartheid. In 1992 she moved to California. Until it's time to go home again, she lives and writes in San Diego. marion is acclaimed in local poetry circles as a performer of original works of poetry and prose, solo and en troupe, in San Diego, Mexico and Los Angeles. Her work is published on walls.

Mike Davis is the author of *City of Quartz, Ecology of Fear, Dead Cities: and Other Tales, Monster at Our Door, Planet of Slums*, and co-author with Jim Miller and Kelly Mayhew of *Under the Perfect Sun: The San Diego Tourists Never See*. He lives in San Diego.

Mark Dery is a cultural critic and the author and editor of several books, most recently, *The Pyrotechnic Insanitarium: American Culture on the Brink* (1999; www.markdery.com). A Chula Vista homeboy, he is currently writing a series of essays on the cultural psyche of San Diego, specifically its borderlands, badlands, and suburban sprawl. Mark is the director of digital journalism at New York University, in the Department of Journalism.

Estela Eaton has been published in *Gut Cult, Pacific Review, Chicago Literary Review,* and *Bordered Sexualities*, an anthology forthcoming from Hyperbole Books. Currently, she lives in Jersey City.

Sharon Elise teaches sociology and ethnic studies courses at a public university, gardens and writes poetry at the home she shares with her husband and her cat a couple miles from the ocean cliffs.

Heather Eudy received her MFA in Creative Writing at San Diego State University and currently teaches English at San Diego City College and Southwestern College.

Mel Freilicher teaches writing and literature at University of California at San Diego and San Diego State University.

reg e. gaines is a poet, writer, and director. He is a 1996 Bessie Award recipient, winner of the 2004 Downtown Urban Theater Festival's *Best Play Award*, a two time Tony Award nominee, a Grammy Award nominee and a finalist in the 2005 Heideman Ten Minute Play Competition. reg's latest book, *2 b*

Blk & wrt. on B.A.G. Lady Press, will be released in spring, 2005.

Harold Jaffe is the author of 11 books, including eight fiction collections and three novels: *15 Serial Killers* (Raw Dog Screaming Press, 2003); False Positive (FC Books, 2002); *Sex for the Millennium* (Black Ice Books, 1999); *Othello Blues* (FictionNet, 1996); *Straight Razor* (Black Ice Books, 1995); *Eros Anti-Eros* (City Lights, 1990); *Madonna and Other Spectacles* (PAJ/FSG, 1988); *Beasts* (Curbstone, 1986); *Dos Indios* (Thunder's Mouth Press, 1983); *Mourning Crazy Horse* (Fiction Collective, 1982); and *Mole's Pity* (Fiction Collective, 1979). Jaffe's fiction has appeared in journals all over the world, and his novels and stories have been translated into German, Japanese, Spanish, French, Dutch, Czech, and Serbo-Croatian. He is editor of *Fiction International* and is a Professor of English who teaches in the MFA Program at San Diego State University.

Ed James is a writer who lives in San Diego.

Jimmy Jazz is the captain of the virtual pirate ship Pirate Enclave (www.onecity.com/pirate). He lives in San Diego.

l.g. kanga has read her work at various venues within the Philadelphia and San Diego areas. She currently resides and teaches in San Diego and will be published in the fall edition of *Chain*.

Steve Kowit received a National Endowment for the Arts Fellowship as well as the *Atlanta Review's* Puamanok Prize for poetry (1996). Since 1990, he has held the position of professor of English at Southwestern College in Chula Vista. His poems have been published in *Poetry Now, Wormwood Review, New York Review,* and *Beloit Poetry Journal,* among others. One of the best-known and most sought after workshop teachers in California, Steve Kowit has written a poetry writing guidebook, *In the Palm of Your Hand,* which is widely used in colleges and universities. His most recent books of poetry include *Passionate Journey: Poems and Drawings in the Erotic Mood* and *The Dumbbell Nebula*.

Susan Luzzaro has published a chapbook titled *Complicity* and a volume of poetry titled *Flesh Envelope,* and she is currently working on a book of essays. She lives in Chula

Vista with her family.

Nadia Mandilawi has lived in San Diego for the past five years. After graduating from San Diego State University with an MFA in 2004 she currently teaches English at San Diego City College.

Hector A. Martinez was born and raised in Los Angeles but has lived in San Diego since 1996. His work has appeared in *Zyzzyva, Quarterly West,* and *Puerto del Sol.* He received an MFA from San Diego State University in 1999 and is currently an Assistant Professor of English at San Diego City College.

Trissy McGhee lives in San Diego and has an MFA in Creative Writing from San Diego State University.

Katherine Melcher is an urban designer and land planner living in San Diego.

minerva was gray when she wrote "The Original Negro Blondes." Bassist Rob Thorsen, who is losing his hair, wrote original music for the poem and the two will record the piece in spring 2005.

d. zenani mzube: woman/writer/mama/student/teacher-on-the-rise, trying to make her rent in san diego. loves to laugh, is compelled to write, is committed to being an artist in times of these wars.

Megan Pincus Kajitani is a writer, editor, advisor, artist, spirited dancer and shower singer who lives in Carlsbad with her adorably tan-lined husband, Alex. She was raised in Orange County and has lived in Washington, D.C., Copenhagen, Denmark, and Madison, Wisconsin, where she earned her M.A. in Communication Arts in 2002.

Karen Lewis recently completed the MFA Program at Antioch-Los Angeles and she leads workshops with California Poets in the Schools. When her father was alive, the family spent many, many summers in San Diego County.

Lance Newman teaches US Literature and Creative Writing at California State University, San Marcos and also guides river trips on the Colorado in Grand Canyon. His poems have appeared in *Beloit Poetry Journal, Poets Against the War, New*

CollAge Magazine, PoetryNet, Perigee, and May Swenson's anthology *American Sports Poems.*

Daniel José Older is a writer, composer and paramedic living in Brooklyn, New York.

David Reid is the editor of *Sex, Death and God in L.A.* His next book will be *The Brazen Age: New York City and the American Empire in the Nineteen-Forties.*

Kate Savage is a writer living in San Diego.

Jensea Storie is the recipient of The First Place Poetry Award at CSU Pomona's 2004 Writing Conference. Her poems have been published in the *Pomona Valley Review,* and she was a candidate at The Community of Writers at Squaw Valley in 2004.

Flavia Tamayo's poetry has appeared in the anthology, *Catena,* and she has forthcoming poetry in the anthology, *L.A. Women of Color: Poetry is Not a Luxury.* She has been a member of the "Women's Poetry Project," based in Silverlake, California, for six years and is also an English instructor at Los Angeles City College where she teaches creative writing, composition, and literature.

Scott Tinley is the author of six books and numerous published works of fiction. His forthcoming novel, *In the Wake of Our Past,* will be published in the summer of 2005. He is a seventh generation Southern Californian and still surfs three hundred days per year near his home in Del Mar. He teaches writing at Grossmont College in the winter and Jr. Lifeguards in the summer.

Perry Vasquez is a visual and conceptual artist living in San Diego where he is a faculty member at Southwestern Community College.

Ioanna Warwick is a widely published and award-winning poet. She has worked as a journalist, editor, translator, and college instructor.

Donna J. Watson aka DJ teaches at San Diego City College and hosts a local writing workshop, the ZHI Spot Writers' Salon in North Park. She was a featured writer for Border

Voices (2003) and her publishing credits include *Nommogeneity: Pot Liquor for Writer's Block* and *Dyna Ho Hums*. Her work has appeared in *Catalyst Magazine, The Drumming Between Us, City Works* and *The Pacific Review*.

Megan Webster is a founding member of San Diego Writers' Cooperative, and she currently teaches creative writing at San Diego Writers, Ink. Her poems have appeared in numerous journals, including *City Works, Cedar Hill Review, California Quarterly, Tidepools* and *ONTHEBUS*.

The editor would like to thank the authors of the following previously published material for donating their work to Sunshine/Noir.

Sandra Alcosser: "Throughout the Duration of the Pulse of a Heart Changes Form" is from *Except by Nature* (1998) on Graywolf Press.

Jimmy Santiago Baca: "Bull's Blood" is from *The Importance of a Piece of Paper* (2004) on Grove Press.

Marilyn Chin: "Where We Live Now" is from *Rhapsody in Plain Yellow* (2002) on W. W. Norton.

Mike Davis: "The Perfect Fire," (2003) first appeared on www.tomdispatch.com, Tom Engelhardt's weblog from the Nation Institute.

Harold Jaffe: "Things to Do During Time of War" (1991) is from *Straight Razor* (1995) on Black Ice Books.

About the Editor

Jim Miller has an MFA in Creative Writing from San Diego State University and a Ph.D. in American Cultural Studies from Bowling Green State University. His first book, *Under the Perfect Sun: The San Diego Tourists Never See* (with Mike Davis and Kelly Mayhew) came out on The New Press in 2003. His next book, entitled *Better To Reign in Hell: Inside the Raiders Fan Empire* (with Kelly Mayhew) is due out on the New Press in the fall of 2005. Miller has published fiction in *Fiction International, New Novel Review, Kiosk, Bakunin, Heaven Bone, Hastings Women's Law Review, Left Curve, Umbrella Magazine*, and *Jack Ruby's Slippers*. His poetry has appeared in *California Quarterly, The Ethiop's Ear, Paterson Literary Review, Cedar Hill Review, Portfolio, The Moment*, and *Pacific Review*. His critical work has been published in *Canon, Science Fiction Studies, Modern Drama, Research and Society, Postmodern Studies, Working Title, A Community of Readers, The Journal of San Diego History, American Book Review, Two Girl's Review*, and the *San Diego Union-Tribune*. He is a Professor of English at San Diego City College.